History of King Richard the Third of England

Makers of History

History of King Richard the Third of England

Makers of History

JACOB ABBOTT

COSIMOCLASSICS

NEW YORK

When the news reached London that the king had
been seized on the way to the capital, and was in Gloucester's
custody, it produced a universal commotion. Queen Elizabeth was
thrown at once into a state of great anxiety and alarm. The tidings
reached her at midnight. She was in the palace at Westminster at
the time. She rose immediately in the greatest terror, and began
to make preparations for fleeing to sanctuary with the Duke of
York, her second son. All her friends in the neighborhood were
aroused and summoned to her aid. The palace soon became
a scene of universal confusion.

—"Taking Sanctuary"

THE ROYAL CHAMPION.

PREFACE.

KING RICHARD THE THIRD, known commonly in history as Richard the Usurper, was perhaps as bad a man as the principle of hereditary sovereignty ever raised to the throne, or perhaps it should rather be said, as the principle of hereditary sovereignty ever *made.* There is no evidence that his natural disposition was marked with any peculiar depravity. He was made reckless, unscrupulous, and cruel by the influences which surrounded him, and the circumstances in which he lived, and by being habituated to believe, from his earliest childhood, that the family to which he belonged were born to live in luxury and splendor, and to reign, while the millions that formed the great mass of the community were created only to toil and to obey. The manner in which the principles of pride, ambition, and desperate love of power, which were instilled into his mind in his earliest years, brought forth in the end their legitimate fruits, is clearly seen by the following narrative.

CONTENTS.

ENGRAVINGS.

Engravings.

KING RICHARD III.

CHAPTER I.

RICHARD'S MOTHER.

The great quarrel between the houses of York and Lancaster.

THE mother of King Richard the Third was
a beautiful, and, in many respects, a noble-
minded woman, though she lived in very rude,
turbulent, and trying times. She was born, so
to speak, into one of the most widely-extended,
the most bitter, and the most fatal of the family
quarrels which have darkened the annals of the
great in the whole history of mankind, namely,
that long-protracted and bitter contest which
was waged for so many years between the two
great branches of the family of Edward the
Third—the houses of York and Lancaster—for
the possession of the kingdom of England.
This dreadful quarrel lasted for more than a
hundred years. It led to wars and commo-
tions, to the sacking and burning of towns, to
the ravaging of fruitful countries, and to atrocious deeds of violence of every sort, almost
without number. The internal peace of hund-

reds of thousands of families all over the land
was destroyed by it for many generations. Husbands were alienated from wives, and parents
from children by it. Murders and assassina-
tions innumerable grew out of it. And what
was it all about? you will ask. It arose from
the fact that the descendants of a certain king
had married and intermarried among each other in such a complicated manner that for several generations nobody could tell which of
two different lines of candidates was fairly entitled to the throne. The question was settled
at last by a prince who inherited the claim on
one side marrying a princess who was the heir
on the other. Thus the conflicting interests of
the two houses were combined, and the quarrel
was ended.

But, while the question was pending, it kept
the country in a state of perpetual commotion,
with feuds, and quarrels, and combats innumerable, and all the other countless and indescrib-
able horrors of civil war.

The two branches of the royal family which
were engaged in this quarrel were called the
houses of York and Lancaster, from the fact
that those were the titles of the fathers and
heads of the two lines respectively. The Lancaster party were the descendants of John of

SCENES OF CIVIL WAR.

Intricate questions of genealogy and descent.

Gaunt, Duke of Lancaster, and the York party
were the successors and heirs of his brother Edmund, Duke of York. These men were both
sons of Edward the Third, the King of England
who reigned immediately before Richard the
Second. A full account of the family is given
in our history of Richard the Second. Of course,
they being brothers, their children were cousins,
and they ought to have lived together in peace
and harmony. And then, besides being related to each other through their fathers, the two
branches of the family intermarried together, so
as to make the relationships in the following
generations so close and so complicated that it
was almost impossible to disentangle them. In
reading the history of those times, we find dukes
or princes fighting each other in the field, or
laying plans to assassinate each other, or striv-
ing to see which should make the other a captive, and shut him up in a dungeon for the rest
of his days; and yet these enemies, so exasperated and implacable, are very near relations—
cousins, perhaps, if the relationship is reckoned
in one way, and uncle and nephew if it is reckoned in another. During the period of this
struggle, all the great personages of the court,
and all, or nearly all, the private families of the
kingdom, and all the towns and the villages,

9—2

were divided and distracted by the dreadful feud.

Richard's mother, whose name, before she was married, was Lady Cecily Neville, was born into one side of this quarrel, and then afterward married into the other side of it. This is a specimen of the way in which the contest became complicated in multitudes of cases. Lady Cecily was descended from the Duke of Lancaster, but she married the Duke of York, in the third generation from the time when the quarrel began.

Of course, upon her marriage, Lady Cecily Neville became the Duchess of York. Her husband was a man of great political importance in his day, and, like the other nobles of the land, was employed continually in wars and in expeditions of various kinds, in the course of which he was continually changing his residence from castle to castle all over England, and sometimes making excursions into Ireland, Scotland, and France. His wife accompanied him in many of these wanderings, and she led, of course, so far as external circumstances were concerned, a wild and adventurous life. She was, however, very quiet and domestic in her tastes, though proud and ambitious in her aspirations, and she occupied herself, wherever she was, in regulating her husband's household, teaching and training her children, and in attending with great regularity and faithfulness to her religious duty, as religious duty was understood in those days.

The following is an account, copied from an ancient record, of the manner in which she spent her days at one of the castles where she was residing.

"She useth to arise at seven of the clock, and hath readye her chapleyne to say with her mattins of the daye (that is, morning prayers), and when she is fully readye, she hath a lowe mass in her chamber. After mass she taketh something to recreate nature, and soe goeth to the chapelle, hearinge the divine service and two lowe masses. From thence to dynner, during the tyme of whih she hath a lecture of holy matter (that is, reading from a religious book), either Hilton of Contemplative and Active Life, or some other spiritual and instructive work. After dynner she giveth audyence to all such as hath any matter to shrive unto her, by the space of one hower, and then sleepeth one quarter of an hower, and after she hath slept she contynueth in prayer until the first peale of even songe.

"In the tyme of supper she reciteth the lec-
2

ture that was had at dynner to those that be in her presence. After supper she disposeth herself to be famyliare with her gentlewomen to the seasoning of honest myrthe, and one hower before her going to bed she taketh a cup of wine, and after that goeth to her pryvie closette, and taketh her leave of God for all nighte, makinge end of her prayers for that daye, and by eighte of the clocke is in bedde."

The going to bed at eight o'clock was in keeping with the other arrangements of the day, for we find by a record of the rules and orders of the duchess's household that the dinner-hour was eleven, and the supper was at four.

This lady, Richard's mother, during her married life, had no less than twelve children. Their names were Anne, Henry, Edward, Edmund, Elizabeth, Margaret, William, John, George, Thomas, Richard, and Ursula. Thus Richard, the subject of this volume, was the eleventh, that is, the last but one. A great many of these, Richard's brothers and sisters, died while they were children. All the boys died thus except four, namely, Edward, Edmund, George, and Richard. Of course, it is only with those four that we have any thing to do in the present narrative.

Several of the other children, however, besides these three, lived for some time. They resided generally with their mother while they were young, but as they grew up they were often separated both from her and from their father—the duke, their father, being often called away from home, in the course of the various wars in which he was engaged, and his wife frequently accompanied him. On such occasions the boys were left at some castle or other, under the care of persons employed to take charge of their education. They used to write letters to their father from time to time, and it is curious that these letters are the earliest examples of letters from children to parents which have been preserved in history. Two of the boys were at one time under the charge of a man named Richard Croft, and the boys thought that he was too strict with them. One of the letters, which has been preserved, was written to complain of this strictness, or, as the boy expressed it, "the odieux rule and demeaning" of their tutor, and also to ask for some "fyne bonnets," which the writer wished to have sent for himself and for his little brother. There is another long letter extant which was written at nearly the same time. This letter was written, or at least signed, by two of the boys, Edward and

Edmund, and was addressed to their father on the occasion of some of his victories. But, though signed by the boys' names, I suspect, from the lofty language in which it is expressed, and from the many high-flown expressions of duty which it contains, that it was really written *for* the boys by their mother or by one of their teachers. Of this, however, the reader can judge for himself on perusing the letter. In this copy the spelling is modernized so as to make it more intelligible, but the language is transcribed exactly from the original.

"Right high and mighty prince, our most worshipful and greatly redoubted lord and father:

"In as lowly a wise as any sons can or may, we recommend us unto your good lordship, and please it to your highness to wit, that we have received your worshipful letters yesterday by your servant William Clinton, bearing date at York, the 29th day of May.*

"By the which William, and by the relation of John Milewater, we conceive your worshipful and victorious speed against your enemies,

* There were no postal arrangements in those days, and all letters were sent by private, and generally by special messengers.

The boys congratulate their father on his victories.

to their great shame, and to us the most comfortable things that we desire to hear. Whereof we thank Almighty God of his gifts, beseeching him heartily to give you that good and cotidian* fortune hereafter to know your enemies, and to have the victory over them.

"And if it please your highness to know of our welfare, at the making of this letter we were in good health of body, thanked be God, beseeching your good and gracious fatherhood for our daily blessing.

"And whereas you command us by your said letters to attend specially to our learning in our young age, that should cause us to grow to honor and worship in our old age, please it your highness to wit, that we have attended to our learning since we came hither, and shall hereafter, by the which we trust to God your gracious lordship and good fatherhood shall be pleased.

"Also we beseech your good lordship that it may please you to send us Harry Lovedeyne, groom of your kitchen, whose service is to us right agreeable; and we will send you John Boyes to wait upon your lordship.

"Right high and mighty prince, our most worshipful and greatly redoubted lord and fa-

* Daily.

ther, we beseech Almighty God to give you as
good life and long as your own princely heart
can best desire.

"Written at your Castle of Ludlow, the 3d
of June.

"Your humble sons,

"E. MARCHE.

"E. RUTLAND."

The subscriptions E. March and E. Rutland
stand for Edward, Earl of March, and Edmund,
Earl of Rutland; for, though these boys were
then only eleven and twelve years of age respectively, they were both earls.   One of them,
afterward, when he was about seventeen years
old, was cruelly killed on the field of battle,
where he had been fighting with his father, as
we shall see in another chapter.   The other,
Edward, became King of England.   He came
immediately before Richard the Third in the
line.

The letter which the boys wrote was super-
scribed as follows :

"To the right high and mighty prince, our
most worshipful and greatly redoubted lord and
father, the Duke of York, Protector and Defender of England."

LUDLOW CASTLE.

The castle of Ludlow, where the boys were residing when this letter was written, was a strong fortress built upon a rock in the western part of England, not far from Shrewsbury. The engraving is a correct representation of it, as it appeared at the period when those boys were there, and it gives a very good idea of the sort of place where kings and princes were accustomed to send their families for safety in those stormy times. Soon after the period of which we are speaking, Ludlow Castle was sacked and destroyed. The ruins of it, however, remain to the present day, and they are visited with much interest by great numbers of modern travelers.

Lady Cecily, as we have already seen, was in many respects a noble woman, and a most faithful and devoted wife and mother; she was, however, of a very lofty and ambitious spirit, and extremely proud of her rank and station. Almost all her brothers and sisters—and the family was very large—were peers and peeresses, and when she married Prince Richard Plantagenet, her heart beat high with exultation and joy to think that she was about to become a queen. She believed that Prince Richard was fully entitled to the throne at that time, for reasons which will be fully explained in the next chapter, and that, even if his claims should

not be recognized until the death of the king
who was then reigning, they certainly would be
so recognized then, and she would become an
acknowledged queen, as she thought she was
already one by right. So she felt greatly exalted in spirit, and moved and acted among all
who surrounded her with an air of stately re-
serve of the most grand and aristocratic character.

In fact, there has, perhaps, no time and place
been known in the history of the world in
which the spirit of aristocracy was more lofty
and overbearing in its character than in England during the period when the Plantagenet
family were in prosperity and power. The nobles formed then, far more strikingly than they
do now, an entirely distinct and exalted class,
that looked down upon all other ranks and gra-
dations of society as infinitely beneath them.
Their only occupation was war, and they regarded all those who were engaged in any em-
ployments whatever, that were connected with
art or industry, with utter disdain. These last
were crowded together in villages and towns
which were formed of dark and narrow streets,
and rude and comfortless dwellings. The nobles lived in grand castles scattered here and
there over the country, with extensive parks

CASTLE AND PARK OF THE MIDDLE AGES.

and pleasure-grounds around them, where they loved to marshal their followers, and inaugurate marauding expeditions against their rivals or their enemies. They were engaged in constant wars and contentions with each other, each thirsting for more power and more splendor than he at present enjoyed, and treating all beneath him with the utmost haughtiness and disdain. Richard's mother exhibited this aristocratic loftiness of spirit in a very high degree, and it was undoubtedly in a great manner through the influence which she exerted over her children that they were inspired with those sentiments of ambition and love of glory to which the crimes and miseries into which several of them fell in their subsequent career were owing.

To assist her in the early education of her children, Richard's mother appointed one of the ladies of the court their governess. This governess was a personage of very high rank, being descended from the royal line. With the ideas which Lady Cecily entertained of the exalted position of her family, and of the future destiny of her children, none but a lady of high rank would be thought worthy of being intrusted with such a charge. The name of the governess was Lady Mortimer.

Sir Richard Croft, the boys' governor.

The boys, as they grew older, were placed
under the charge of a governor. His name was
Sir Richard Croft. It is this Sir Richard that
they allude to in their letter. He, too, was a
person of high rank and of great military distinction. The boys, however, thought him too
strict and severe with them; at least so it would
seem, from the manner in which they speak of
him in the letter.

The governor and the governess appear to
have liked each other very well, for after a time
Sir Richard offered himself to Lady Mortimer,
and they were married.

Besides Ludlow Castle, Prince Richard had
several other strongholds, where his wife from
time to time resided. Richard, who was one
of the youngest of the children, was born at
one of these, called Fotheringay Castle; but,
before coming to the event of his birth, I must
give some account of the history and fortunes
of his father.

RICHARD'S FATHER. 33

Genealogy of Richard Plantagenet.   Family of Edward III.

CHAPTER II.
RICHARD'S FATHER.

RICHARD'S father was a prince of the house of York. In the course of his life he was declared heir to the crown, but he died before he attained possession of it, thus leaving it for his children. The nature of his claim to the crown, and, indeed, the general relation of the various branches of the family to each other, will be seen by the genealogical table on the next page but one.

Edward the Third, who reigned more than one hundred years before Richard the Third, and his queen Philippa, left at their decease four sons, as appears by the table.* They had other children besides these, but it was only these four, namely, Edward, Lionel, John, and Edmund, whose descendants were involved in the quarrels for the succession. The others either died young, or else, if they arrived at maturity, the lines descending from them soon became extinct.

Of the four that survived, the oldest was Ed-

* See page 35.

ward, called in history the Black Prince. A full account of his life and adventures is given in our history of Richard the Second. He died before his father, and so did not attain to the crown. He, however, left his son Richard his heir, and at Edward's death Richard became king. Richard reigned twenty years, and then, in consequence of his numerous vices and crimes, and of his general mismanagement, he was deposed, and Henry, the son of John of Gaunt, Duke of Lancaster, Edward's third son, ascended the throne in his stead.

Now, as appears by the table, John of Gaunt was the third of the four sons, Lionel, Duke of Clarence, being the second. The descendants of Lionel would properly have come before those of John in the succession, but it happen-ed that the only descendants of Lionel were Philippa, a daughter, and Roger, a grandchild, who was at this time an infant. Neither of these were able to assert their claims, although in theory their claims were acknowledged to be prior to those of the descendants of John. The people of England, however, were so desir-ous to be rid of Richard, that they were will-ing to submit to the reign of any member of the royal family who should prove strong enough to dispossess him. So they accepted

Genealogical table of the houses of York and Lancaster.

GENEALOGICAL TABLE OF THE FAMILY OF EDWARD III., SHOWING THE CONNECTION OF THE HOUSES OF YORK AND LANCASTER.

EDWARD III.=Philippa.

EDWARD (The Black Prince).
RICHARD II.

LIONEL (Duke of Clarence).
PHILIPPA=Edward Mortimer.
ROGER MORTIMER (Earl of March).
ANNE=Richard of York. (See fourth column.)

JOHN (Of Gaunt, Duke of Lancaster).
HENRY IV.
HENRY V.
HENRY VI.
EDWARD (Prince of Wales).

EDMUND (Duke of York).
RICHARD=Anne. (See second column.)
RICHARD PLANTAGENET (Duke of York).
EDWARD IV. GEORGE (Duke of Clarence). RICHARD III.

The character = denotes marriage; the short perpendicular line | a descent. There were many other children and descendants in the different branches of the family besides those whose names are inserted in the table. The table includes only those essential to an understanding of the history.

Henry of Lancaster, who ascended the throne
as Henry the Fourth, and he and his successors
in the Lancastrian line, Henry the Fifth and
Henry the Sixth, held the throne for many
years.

Still, though the people of England generally acquiesced in this, the families of the other
brothers, namely, of Lionel and Edmund, called
generally the houses of Clarence and of York,
were not satisfied. They combined together,
and formed a great many plots and conspiracies against the house of Lancaster, and many
insurrections and wars, and many cruel deeds
of violence and murder grew out of the quarrel. At length, to strengthen their alliance
more fully, Richard, the second son of Edmund
of York, married Anne, a descendant of the
Clarence line. The other children, who came
before these, in the two lines, soon afterward
died, leaving the inheritance of both to this pair.
Their son was Richard, the father of Richard
the Third. He is called Richard Plantagenet,
Duke of York. On the death of his father and
mother, he, of course, became the heir not only
of the immense estates and baronial rights of
both the lines from which he had descended,
but also of the claims of the older line to the
crown of England.

The successive generations of these three lines, down to the period of the union of the second and fourth, cutting off the third, is shown clearly in the table.

Of course, the Lancaster line were much alarmed at the combination of the claims of their rivals. King Henry the Fifth was at that period on the throne, and, by the time that Richard Plantagenet was three years old, under pretense of protecting him from danger, he caused him to be shut up in a castle, and kept a close prisoner there.

Time rolled on. King Henry the Fifth died, and Henry the Sixth succeeded him. Richard Plantagenet was still watched and guarded; but at length, by the time that Richard was thirteen years old, the power and influence of his branch of the royal family, or rather those of the two branches from which, combined, he was descended, were found to be increasing, while that of the house of Lancaster was declining. After a time he was brought out from his imprisonment, and restored to his rank and station. King Henry the Sixth was a man of a very weak and timid mind. He was quite young too, being, in fact, a mere child when he began to reign, and every thing went wrong with his government. While he was young, he

could, of course, do nothing, and when he grew
older he was too gentle and forbearing to control the rough and turbulent spirits around him.
He had no taste for war and bloodshed, but
loved retirement and seclusion, and, as he advanced in years, he fell into the habit of spend-
ing a great deal of his time in acts of piety and
devotion, performed according to the ideas and
customs of the times. The annexed engraving,
representing him as he appeared when he was

HENRY VI. IN HIS CHILDHOOD.

a boy, is copied from the ancient portraits, and well expresses the mild and gentle traits which marked his disposition and character.

Such being the disposition and character of Henry, every thing during his reign went wrong, and this state of things, growing worse and worse as he advanced in life, greatly encouraged and strengthened the house of York in the effort which they were inclined to make to bring their own branch of the family to the throne.

" See," said they, " what we come to by allowing a line of usurpers to reign. These Henrys of Lancaster are all descended from a younger son, while the heirs of the older are living, and have a right to the throne. Richard Plantagenet is the true and proper heir. He is a man of energy. Let us make him king."

But the people of England, though they gradually came to desire the change, were not willing yet to plunge the country again into a state of civil war for the purpose of making it. They would not disturb Henry, they said, while he continued to live; but there was nobody to succeed him, and, when he died, Richard Plantagenet should be king.

Henry was married at this time, but he had no children. The name of his wife was Margaret of Anjou. She was a very extraordinary and celebrated woman. Though very beautiful in person, she was as energetic and masculine in character as her poor husband was effeminate and weak, and she took every thing

QUEEN MARGARET OF ANJOU, WIFE OF HENRY VI.

into her own hands. This, however, made matters worse instead of better, and the whole coun-

try seemed to rejoice that she had no children, for thus, on the death of Henry, the line would become extinct, and Richard Plantagenet and his descendants would succeed, as a matter of course, in a quiet and peaceful manner. As Henry and Margaret had now been married eight or nine years without any children, it was supposed that they never would have any.

Accordingly, Richard Plantagenet was universally looked upon as Henry's successor, and the time seemed to be drawing nigh when the change of dynasty was to take place. Henry's health was very feeble. He seemed to be rapidly declining. His mind was affected, too, quite seriously, and he sometimes sank into a species of torpor from which nothing could arouse him.

Indeed, it became difficult to carry on the government in his name, for the king sank at last into such a state of imbecility that it was impossible to obtain from him the least sign or token that would serve, even for form's sake, as an assent on his part to the royal decrees. At one time Parliament appointed a commission to visit him in his chamber, for the purpose of ascertaining the state that he was in, and to see also whether they could not get some token from him which they could consider as his as-

sent to certain measures which it was deemed
important to take; but they could not get from
the king any answer or sign of any kind, notwithstanding all that they could do or say.
They retired for a time, and afterward came
back again to make a second attempt, and then,
as an ancient narrative records the story, "they
moved and stirred him by all the ways and
means that they could think of to have an answer of the said matter, but they could have no
answer, word nor sign, and therefore, with sor-.
rowful hearts, came away."

This being the state of things, Parliament
thought it time to make some definite arrangements for the succession. Accordingly, they
passed a formal and solemn enactment declaring Richard Plantagenet heir presumptive of
the crown, and investing him with the rank and
privileges pertaining to that position. They
also appointed him, for the present, Protector
and defender of the realm.

Richard, the subject of this volume, was at
this time an infant two years old. The other
ten children had been born at various periods
before.

It was now, of course, expected that Henry
would soon die, and that then Richard Plantagenet would at once ascend the throne, ac-

knowledged by the whole realm as the sole and
rightful heir. But these expectations were suddenly disturbed, and the whole kingdom was
thrown into a state of great excitement and
alarm by the news of a very unexpected and
important event which occurred at this time,
namely, the birth of a child to Margaret, the
queen. This event awakened all the latent
fires of civil dissension and discord anew. The
Lancastrian party, of course, at once rallied
around the infant prince, who, they claimed,
was the rightful heir to the crown. They began at once to reconstruct and strengthen their
plans, and to shape their measures with a view
to retain the kingdom in the Lancaster line.
On the other hand, the friends of the combined
houses of Clarence and York declared that they
would not acknowledge the new-comer as the
rightful heir. They did not believe that he was
the son of the king, for he, as they said, had
been for a long time as good as dead. Some
said that they did not even believe that the
child was Margaret's son. There was a story
that she had had a child, but that he was very
weak and puny, and that he had died soon after his birth, and that Margaret had cunningly
substituted another child in his place, in order
to retain her position and power by having a

supposed son of hers reign as king after her husband should die. Margaret was a woman of so
ambitious and unscrupulous a character, that
she was generally believed capable of adopting
any measures, however criminal and bold, to
accomplish her ends.

But, notwithstanding these rumors, Parliament acknowledged the infant as his father's
son and heir. He was named Edward, and created at once Prince of Wales, which act was a
solemn acknowledgment of his right to the succession. Prince Richard made no open opposition to this; for, although he and his friends
maintained that he had a right to the crown,
they thought that the time had not yet come
for openly advancing their claim, so for the present they determined to be quiet. The child
might not survive, and his father, the king, being in so helpless and precarious a condition,
might cease to live at any time; and if it should
so happen that both the father and the child
should die, Richard would, of course, succeed at
once, without any question. He accordingly
thought it best to wait a little while, and see
what turn things would take.

He soon found that things were taking the
wrong turn. The child lived, and appeared
likely to continue to live, and, what was per-

haps worse for him, the king, instead of declining more and more, began to revive. In a short time he was able to attend to business again, at least so far as to express his assent to measures prepared for him by his ministers. Prince Richard was accordingly called upon to resign his protectorate. He thought it best to yield to this proposal, and he did so, and thus the government was once more in Henry's hands.

Things went on in this way for two or three years, but the breach between the two great parties was all the time widening. Difficulties multiplied in number and increased in magnitude. The country took sides. Armed forces were organized on one side and on the other, and at length Prince Richard openly claimed the crown as his right. This led to a long and violent discussion in Parliament. The result was, that a majority was obtained to vote in favor of Prince Richard's right. The Parliament decreed, however, that the existing state of things should not be disturbed so long as Henry continued to live, but that at Henry's death the crown should descend, not to little Edward his son, the infant Prince of Wales, but to Prince Richard Plantagenet and his descendants forever.

Queen Margaret was at this time at a castle

in Wales, where she had gone with the child, in order to keep him in a place of safety while these stormy discussions were pending. When she heard that Parliament had passed a law setting aside the claims of her child, she declared that she would never submit to it. She immediately sent messengers all over the northern part of the kingdom, summoning the faithful followers of the king every where to arm themselves and assemble near the frontier. She herself went to Scotland to ask for aid. The King of Scotland at that time was a child, but he was related to the Lancastrian family, his grandmother having been a descendant of John of Gaunt, the head of the Lancaster line. He was too young to take any part in the war, but his mother, who was acting as regent, furnished Margaret with troops. Margaret, putting herself at the head of these forces, marched across the frontier into England, and joined herself there to the other forces which had assembled in answer to her summons.

In the mean time, Prince Richard had assembled his adherents too, and had commenced his march to the northward to meet his enemies. He took his two oldest sons with him, the two that wrote the letter quoted in the last chapter. One of these you will recollect was Edward,

Earl of Marche, and the second was Edmund, Earl of Rutland. Edward was now about eighteen years of age, and his brother Edmund about seventeen. One would have said that at this period of life they were altogether too young to be exposed to the hardships, fatigues, and dangers of a martial campaign; but it was the custom in those times for princes and nobles to be taken with their fathers to fields of battle at a very early age. And these youthful warriors were really of great service too, for the interest which they inspired among all ranks of the army was so great, especially when their rank was very high, that they were often the means of greatly increasing the numbers and the enthusiasm of their fathers' followers.

Edward, indeed, was in this instance deemed old enough to be sent off on an independent service, and so, while the prince moved forward with the main body of his army toward the north, he dispatched Edward, accompanied by a suitable escort, to the westward, toward the frontiers of Wales, to assemble all the armed men that he could find in that part of the kingdom who were disposed to espouse his cause. Edmund, who was a year younger than Edward, went with his father.

The prince proceeded to the city of York,

which was then a fortified place of great strength.
The engraving gives a very good idea of the
appearance of the walls in those times. These
walls remain, indeed, almost entire at the present day, and they are visited a great deal by
tourists and travelers, being regarded with much
interest as furnishing a very complete and well-
preserved specimen of the mural fortifications
of the Middle Ages. Such walls, however,
would be almost entirely useless now as means
of defense, since they would not stand at all
against an attack from modern artillery.

The great church seen over the walls, in the
heart of the city, is the famous York minster,
one of the grandest Cathedral churches in England. It was a hundred and fifty years in
building, and it was completed about two cen-
turies before Richard's day.

When Prince Richard reached York, he entered the town, and established himself there,
with a view of waiting till his son should arrive with the re-enforcements which he had
been sent to seek in the western part of England.

While he was there, and before the re-enforcements came, the queen, at the head of her army
from Scotland, which was strengthened, moreover, by the troops which she had obtained in
the north of England, came marching on down

WALLS OF YORK.

9—4

the country in great force. When she came
into the neighborhood of York, she encamped,
and then sent messengers to Prince Richard,
taunting and deriding him for having shut himself up within fortified walls, and daring him to
come out into the open field and fight her.

The prince's counselors advised him to do no
such thing. One of them in particular, a certain Sir Davy Hall, who was an old and faithful officer in the prince's service, urged him to
pay no attention to Queen Margaret's taunts.

"We are not strong enough yet," said he,
"to meet the army which she has assembled.
We must wait till our re-enforcements come.
By going out now we shall put our cause in
great peril, and all to no purpose whatever."

"Ah! Davy, Davy," said the prince, "hast
thou loved me so long, and now wouldst thou
have me dishonored? When I was regent in
Normandy, thou never sawest me keep fortress,
even when the dauphin himself, with all his
power, came to besiege me.* I always, like a
man, came forth to meet him, instead of remaining within my walls, like a bird shut up in a

---

* In former years Prince Richard had acted as viceroy of
the English possessions in France, under King Henry, and
while there he had been engaged in wars with the King of
France, and with the dauphin, his son.

cage. Now if I did not then keep myself shut
up for. fear of a great, strong prince, do you
think I will now, for dread of a scolding woman,
whose weapons are only her tongue and her
nails, and thus give people occasion to say that
I turned dastard before a woman, when no man
had ever been able to make me fear? No,
I will never submit to such disgrace. I would
rather die in honor than live in shame; and
so the great numbers of our enemies do not de-
ter me in the least; they rather encourage me;
therefore, in the name of God and St. George,
advance my banner, for I am determined that I
will go out and fight them, if I go alone."

So Prince Richard came forth from the gates
of York at the head of his columns, and rode on
toward the queen's camp. Edmund went with
him. Edmund was under the care of his tutor,
Robert Aspell, who was charged to keep close
to his side, and to watch over him in the most
vigilant manner. The army of the queen was
at some distance from York, at a place called
Wakefield. Both parties, as is usual in civil
wars, were extremely exasperated against each
other, and the battle was desperately fought.
It was very brief, however, and Richard's troops
were defeated. Richard himself was taken prisoner. Edmund endeavored to escape. His

LAST HOURS OF KING RICHARD'S FATHER.

tutor endeavored to hurry him off the field, but he was stopped on the way by a certain nobleman of the queen's party, named Lord Clifford. The poor boy begged hard for mercy, but Clifford killed him on the spot.

The prince's army, when they found that the battle had gone against them, and that their captain was a prisoner, fled in all directions over the surrounding country, leaving great numbers dead upon the field. The prince himself, as soon as he was taken, was disarmed on the field, and all the leaders of the queen's army, including, as the most authentic accounts relate, the queen herself, gathered around him in wild exultation. They carried him to a mound formed by an ant-hill, which they said, in mockery, should be his throne. They placed him upon it with taunts and derision. They made a crown for him of knotted grass, and put it upon his head, and then made mock obeisances before him, saying, "Hail! king without a kingdom. Hail! prince, without a people."

After having satisfied themselves with their taunts and revilings, the party killed their prisoner and cut off his head. They set his head upon the point of a lance, and in this way presented it to Queen Margaret. The queen ordered the head to be decorated with a paper crown, and then to be carried to York, and set up at the gates of that city upon a tall pole.

Thus was little Richard, the subject of this narrative, left fatherless. He was at this period between eight and nine years old.

CHAPTER III.

THE CHILDHOOD OF RICHARD III.

YOUNG Richard, as was said at the close of the last chapter, was of a very tender age when his father and his brother Edmund were killed at the battle of Wakefield. He was at that time only about eight years old. It is very evident too, from what has been already related of the history of his father and mother, that during the whole period of his childhood and youth he must have passed through very stormy times. It is only a small portion of the life of excitement, conflict, and alarm which was led by his father that there is space to describe in this volume. So unsettled and wandering a life did his father and mother lead, that it is not quite certain in which of the various towns and castles that from time to time they made their residence, he was born. It is supposed, however, that he was born in the Castle of Fotheringay, in the year 1452. His father was killed in 1461, which would make Richard, as has already been said, about eight or nine years old at that time.

There were a great many strange tales related in subsequent years in respect to Richard's birth. He became such a monster, morally, when he grew to be a man, that the people
believed that he was born a monster in person.
The story was that he came into the world very
ugly in face and distorted in form, and that his
hair and his teeth were already grown. These
were considered as portents of the ferociousness
of temper and character which he was subsequently to manifest, and of the unnatural and
cruel crimes which he would live to commit.
It is very doubtful, however, whether any of
these stories are true. It is most probable that
at his birth he looked like any other child.

There were a great many periods of intense
excitement and terror in the family history before the great final calamity at Wakefield when
Richard's father and his brother Edmund were
killed. At these times the sole reliance of the
prince in respect to the care of the younger
children was upon Lady Cecily, their mother.
The older sons went with their father on the
various martial expeditions in which he was engaged. They shared with him the hardships
and dangers of his conflicts, and the triumph
and exultations of his victories. The younger
children, however, remained in seclusion with

their mother, sometimes in one place and sometimes in another, wherever there was, for the
time being, the greatest promise of security.

Indeed, during the early childhood of Richard, the changes and vicissitudes through which
the family passed were so sudden and violent
in their character as sometimes to surpass the
most romantic tales of fiction. At one time,
while Lady Cecily was residing at the Castle of
Ludlow with Richard and some of the younger
children, a party of her husband's enemies, the
Lancastrians, appeared suddenly at the gates of
the town, and, before Prince Richard's party
had time to take any efficient measures for defense, the town and the castle were both taken.
The Lancastrians had expected to find Prince
Richard himself in the castle, but he was not
there. They were exasperated by their disappointment, and in their fury they proceeded to
ransack all the rooms, and to destroy every
thing that came into their hánds. In some of
the inner and more private apartments they
found Lady Cecily and her children. They
immediately seized them all, made them prisoners, and carried them away. By King Henry's orders, they were placed in close custody
in another castle in the southern part of England, and all the property, both of the prince

and of Lady Cecily, was confiscated. While
the mother and the younger children were thus
closely shut up and reduced to helpless destitution, the father and the older sons were obliged
to fly from the country to save their lives. In
less than three months after this time these
same exiled and apparently ruined fugitives
were marching triumphantly through the country, at the head of victorious troops, carrying
all before them. Lady Cecily and her children
were set at liberty, and restored to their property and their rights, while King Henry himself, whose captives they had been, was himself
made captive, and brought in durance to London, and Queen Margaret and her son were in
their turn compelled to fly from the realm to
save their lives.

This last change in the condition of public
affairs took place only a short time before the
great final contest between Prince Richard of
York, King Richard's father, and the family of
Henry, when the prince lost his life at Wakefield, as described in the last chapter.

Of course, young Richard, being brought up
amid these scenes of wild commotion, and accustomed from childhood to witness the most
cruel and remorseless conflicts between branches of the same family, was trained by them to

A HOUSE AND GARDEN BELONGING TO THE HOUSE OF YORK.

be ambitious, daring, and unscrupulous in respect to the means to be used in circumventing
or destroying an enemy. The seed thus sown
produced in subsequent years most dreadful
fruit, as will be seen more fully in the sequel
of his history.

There were a great many hereditary castles
belonging to the family of York, many of which
had descended from father to son for many generations. Some of these castles were strong fortresses, built in wild and inaccessible retreats,
and intended to be used as places of temporary
refuge, or as the rallying-points and rendez-
vous of bodies of armed men. Others were
better adapted for the purposes of a private residence, being built with some degree of refer-
ence to the comfort of the inmates, and surrounded with gardens and grounds, where the
ladies and the children who were left in them
could find recreation and amusement adapted
to their age and sex.

It was in such a castle as this, near London,
that Lady Cecily and her younger children were
residing when her husband went to the northward to meet the forces of the queen, as related
in the last chapter. Here Lady Cecily lived in
great state, for she thought the time was drawing nigh when her husband would be raised to

the throne. Indeed, she considered him as already the true and rightful sovereign of the realm, and she believed that the hour would very soon come when his claims would be universally acknowledged, and when she herself would be Queen of England, and her boys royal princes, and, as such, the objects of universal attention and regard. She instilled these ideas continually into the minds of the children, and she exacted the utmost degree of subserviency and submission toward herself and toward them on the part of all around her.

While she was thus situated in her palace near London, awaiting every day the arrival of a messenger from the north announcing the final victory of her husband over all his foes, she was one day thunderstruck, and overwhelmed with grief and despair, by the tidings that her husband had been defeated, and that he himself, and the dear son who had accompanied him, and was just arriving at maturity, had been ignominiously slain. The queen, too, her most bitter foe, now exultant and victorious, was advancing triumphantly toward London.

Not a moment was to be lost. Lady Cecily had with her, at this time, her two youngest sons, George and Richard. She made immediate arrangements for her flight. It happened that the Earl of Warwick, who was at this time the Lord High Admiral, and who, of course, had command of the seas between England and the Continent, was a relative and friend of Lady Cecily's. He was at this time in London. Lady Cecily applied to him to assist her in making her escape. He consented, and, with his aid, she herself, with her two children and a small number of attendants, escaped secretly from London, and made their way to the southern coast. There Lady Cecily put the children and the attendants on board a vessel, by which they were conveyed to the coast of Holland. On landing there, they were received by the prince of the country, who was a friend of Lady Cecily, and to whose care she commended them. The prince received them with great kindness, and sent them to the city of Utrecht, where he established them safely in one of his palaces, and appointed suitable tutors and governors to superintend their education. Here it was expected that they would remain for several years.

Their mother did not go with them to Holland. Her fears in respect to remaining in England were not for herself, but only for her helpless children. For herself, her only impulse was to face and brave the dangers which threatened her, and triumph over them. So she went boldly back to London, to await there whatever might occur.

Besides, her oldest son was still in England, and she could not forsake him. You will recollect that, when his father went north to meet the forces of Queen Margaret, he sent his oldest son, Edward, Earl of Marche, to the western part of England, to obtain re-enforcements. Edward was at Gloucester when the tidings came to him of his father's death. Gloucester is on the western confines of England, near the southeastern borders of Wales. Now, of course, since her husband was dead, all Lady Cecily's ambition, and all her hopes of revenge were concentrated in him. She wished to be at hand to counsel him, and to co-operate with him by all the means in her power. How she succeeded in these plans, and how, by means of them, he soon became King of England, will appear in the next chapter.

CHAPTER IV.

ACCESSION OF EDWARD IV., RICHARD'S ELDER BROTHER.

RICHARD'S brother Edward, as has already been remarked, was at Gloucester when he heard the news of his father death. This news, of course, made a great change in his condition. To his mother, the event was purely and simply a calamity, and it could awaken no feelings in her heart but those of sorrow and chagrin. In Edward's mind, on the other hand, the first emotions of astonishment and grief were followed immediately by a burst of exultation and pride. He, of course, as now the oldest surviving son, succeeded at once to all the rights and titles which his father had enjoyed, and among these, according to the ideas which his mother had instilled into his mind, was the right to the crown. His heart, therefore, when the first feeling of grief for the loss of his father had subsided, bounded with joy as he exclaimed,

"So now *I* am the King of England."

The enthusiasm which he felt extended itself

5

at once to all around him.　He immediately
made preparations to put himself at the head of
his troops, and march to the eastward, so as to
intercept Queen Margaret on her way to London,
for he knew that she would, of course, now press
forward toward the capital as fast as possible.

He accordingly set out at once upon his
march, and, as he went on, he found that the
number of his followers increased very rapidly.
The truth was, that the queen's party, by their
murder of Richard, and of young Edmund his
son, had gone altogether too far for the good of
their own cause.　The people, when they heard
the tidings, were indignant at such cruelty.
Those who belonged to the party of the house
of York, instead of being intimidated by the severity of the measure, were exasperated at the
brutality of it, and they were all eager to join
the young duke, Edward, and help him to
avenge his father's and his brother's death.
Those who had been before on the side of the
house of Lancaster were discouraged and re-
pelled, while those who had been doubtful were
now ready to declare against the queen.

It is in this way that all excesses in the hour
of victory defeat the very ends they were intended to subserve.　They weaken the perpe-
trators, and not the subjects of them.

In the mean time, while young Edward, at
the head of his army, was marching on from
the westward toward London to intercept the
queen, the Earl of Warwick, who has already
been mentioned as a friend of Lady Cecily, had
also assembled a large force near London, and
he was now advancing toward the northward.
The poor king was with him. Nominally, the
king was in command of the expedition, and
every thing was done in his name, but really
he was a forlorn and helpless prisoner, forced
wholly against his will—so far as the feeble degree of intellect which remained to him enabled
him to exercise a will—to seem to head an enterprise directed against his own wife, and his
best and strongest friend.

The armies of the queen and of the Earl of
Warwick advanced toward each other, until
they met at last at a short distance north of
London. A desperate battle was fought, and
the queen's party were completely victorious.
When night came on, the Earl of Warwick
found that he was beaten at every point, and
that his troops had fled in all directions, leaving
thousands of the dead and dying all along the
road sides. The camp had been abandoned, and
there was no time to save any thing; even the
poor king was left behind, and the officers of

the queen's army found him in a tent, with only
one attendant. Of course, the queen was over-
joyed at recovering possession of her husband,
not merely on his own account personally, but
also because she could now act again directly
in his name. So she prepared a proclamation,
by which the king revoked all that he had
done while in the hands of Warwick, on the
ground that he had been in durance, and had
not acted of his own free will, and also declared
Edward a traitor, and offered a large reward for
his apprehension.

The queen was now once more filled with
exultation and joy. Her joy would have been
complete were it not that Edward himself was
still to be met, for he was all this time advancing from the westward; she, however, thought
that there was not much to be feared from such
a boy, Edward being at this time only about
nineteen years of age. So the queen moved on
toward London, flushed with the victory, and
exasperated with the opposition which she had
met with. Her soldiers were under very little
control, and they committed great excesses.
They ravaged the country, and plundered without mercy all those whom they considered as
belonging to the opposite party; they committed, too, many atrocious acts of cruelty. It is

always thus in civil war.　In foreign wars, armies are much more easily kept under control. Troops march through a foreign territory, feeling no personal spite or hatred against the inhabitants of it, for they think it is a matter of course that the people should defend their country and resist invaders.　But in a civil war, the men of each party feel a special personal hate against every individual that does not belong to their side, and in periods of actual conflict this hatred becomes a rage that is perfectly uncontrollable.

Accordingly, as the queen and her troops advanced, they robbed and murdered all who came in their way, and they filled the whole country with terror.　They even seized and plundered a convent, which was a species of sacrilege. This greatly increased the general alarm.　"The wretches!" exclaimed the people, when they heard the tidings, "nothing is sacred in their eyes."　The people of London were particularly alarmed.　They thought there was danger that the city itself would be given up to plunder if the queen's troops gained admission.　So they all turned against her.　She sent one day into the town for a supply of provisions, and the authorities, perhaps thinking themselves bound by their official duty to obey orders of this kind coming in the king's name, loaded up some wagons and sent them forth, but the people raised a mob, and stopped the wagons at the gates, refusing to let them go on.

In the mean time, Edward, growing every hour stronger as he advanced, came rapidly on toward London. He was joined at length by the Earl of Warwick and the remnant of the force which remained to the earl after the battle which he had fought with the queen. The queen, now finding that Edward's strength was becoming formidable, did not dare to meet him; so she retreated toward the north again. Edward, instead of pursuing her, advanced directly toward London. The people threw open the gates to him, and welcomed him as their deliverer. They thronged the streets to look upon him as he passed, and made the air ring with their loud and long acclamations.

There was, indeed, every thing in the circumstances of the case to awaken excitement and emotion. Here was a boy not yet out of his teens, extremely handsome in appearance and agreeable in manners, who had taken the field in command of a very large force to avenge the cruel death of his father and brother, and was now coming boldly, at the head of his troops, into the very capital of the king and queen un-

der whose authority his father and brother had been killed.

The most extraordinary circumstance connected with these proceedings was, that during all this time Henry was still acknowledged by every one as the actual king. Edward and his friends maintained, indeed, that he, Edward, was *entitled* to reign, but no one pretended that any thing had yet been done which could have the legal effect of putting him upon the throne. There was, however, now a general expectation that the time for the formal deposition of Henry was near, and in and around London all was excitement and confusion. The people from the surrounding towns flocked every day into the city to see what they could see, and to hear what they could hear. They thronged the streets whenever Edward appeared in public, eager to obtain a glimpse of him.

At length, a few days after Edward entered the city, his counselors and friends deemed that the time had come for action. Accordingly, they made arrangements for a grand review in a large open field. Their design was by this review to call together a great concourse of spectators. A vast assembly convened according to their expectations. In the midst of the ceremonies, two noblemen appeared before the multitude to make addresses to them. One of them made a speech in respect to Henry, denouncing the crimes, and the acts of treachery and of oppression which his government had committed. He dilated long on the feebleness and incapacity of the king, and his total inability to exercise any control in the management of public affairs. After he had finished, he called out to the people in a loud voice to declare whether they would submit any longer to have such a man for king.

The people answered "NAY, NAY, NAY," with loud and long acclamations.

Then the other speaker made an address in favor of Edward. He explained at length the nature of his title to the crown, showing it to be altogether superior in point of right to that of Henry. He also spoke long and eloquently in praise of Edward's personal qualifications, describing his courage, his activity, and energy, and the various graces and accomplishments for which he was distinguished, in the most glowing terms. He ended by demanding of the people whether they would have Edward for king.

The people answered "YEA, YEA, YEA; KING EDWARD FOREVER! KING EDWARD FOREVER!" with acclamations as long and loud as before.

Of course there could be no legal validity in such proceedings as these, for, even if England had at that time been an elective monarchy, the acclamations of an accidental assembly drawn together to witness a review could on no account have been deemed a valid vote. This ceremony was only meant as a very public announcement of the intention of Edward immediately to assume the throne.

The next day, accordingly, a grand council was held of all the great barons, and nobles, and officers of state. By this council a decree was passed that King Henry, by his late proceedings, had forfeited the crown, and Edward was solemnly declared king in his stead. Immediately afterward, Edward rode at the head of a royal procession, which was arranged for the purpose, to Westminster, and there, in the presence of a vast assembly, he took his seat upon the throne. While there seated, he made a speech to the audience, in which he explained the nature of his hereditary rights, and declared his intention to maintain his rights thenceforth in the most determined manner.

The king now proceeded to Westminster Abbey, where he performed the same ceremonies a second time. He was also publicly proclaimed king on the same day in various parts of London.

Edward was now full of ardor and enthusiasm, and his first impulse was to set off, at the
head of his army, toward the north, in pursuit
of the queen and the old king. The king and
queen had gone to York. The queen had not
only the king under her care, but also her son,
the little Prince of Wales, who was now about
eight years old. This young prince was the
heir to the crown on the Lancastrian side, and
Edward was, of course, very desirous of getting
him, as well as the king and queen, into his
hands; so he put himself at the head of his
troops, and began to move forward as fast as he
could go. The body of troops under his command consisted of fifty thousand men. In the
queen's army, which was encamped in the neighborhood of York, there were about sixty thousand.

Both parties were extremely exasperated
against each other, and were eager for the fight.
Edward gave orders to his troops to grant no
quarter, but, in the event of victory, to massa-
cre without mercy every man that they could
bring within their reach. The armies came together at a place called Towton. The combat
was begun in the midst of a snow-storm. The
armies fought from nine o'clock in the morn-
ning till three in the afternoon, and by that

time the queen's troops were every where driven from the field. Edward's men pursued them along the roads, slaughtering them without mercy as fast as they could overtake them, until at length nearly forty thousand men were left dead upon the ground.

The queen fled toward the north, taking with her her husband and child. Edward entered York in triumph. At the gates he found the head of his father and that of his brother still remaining upon the poles where the queen had put them. He took them reverently down, and then put other heads in their places, which he cut off for the purpose from some of his prisoners. He was in such a state of fury, that I suppose, if he could have caught the king and queen, he would have cut off *their* heads, and put them on the poles in the place of his father's and his brother's; but he could not catch them. They fled to the north, toward the frontiers of Scotland, and so escaped from his hands.

Edward determined not to pursue the fugitives any farther at that time, as there were many important affairs to be attended to in London, and so he concluded to be satisfied at present with the victory which he had obtained, and with the dispersion of his enemies, and to return to the capital. He first, however,

gathered together the remains of his father and
brother, and caused them to be buried with solemn funeral ceremonies in one of his castles
near York. This was, however, only a temporary arrangement, for, as soon as his affairs were
fully settled, the remains were disinterred, and
conveyed, with great funeral pomp and parade,
to their final resting-place in the southern part
of the kingdom.

As soon as Edward reached London, one of
the first things that he did was to send for his
two brothers, George and Richard, who, as will
be recollected, had been removed by their mother to Holland, and were now in Utrecht pursuing their education. These two boys were all the
brothers of Edward that remained now alive.
They came back to London. Their widowed
mother's heart was filled with a melancholy
sort of joy in seeing her children once more together, safe in their native land; but her spirit,
after reviving for a moment, sank again, overwhelmed with the bitter and irreparable loss
which she had sustained in the death of her
husband. His death was, of course, a fatal blow
to all those ambitious plans and aspirations
which she had cherished for herself. Though
the mother of a king, she could now never become herself a queen; and, disappointed and un-

happy, she retired to one of the family castles
in the neighborhood of London, and lived there
comparatively alone and in great seclusion.

The boys, on the other hand, were brought
forward very conspicuously into public life. In
the autumn of the same year in which Edward
took possession of the crown, they were made
royal dukes, with great parade and ceremony,
and were endowed with immense estates to enable them to support the dignity of their rank
and position. George was made Duke of Clarence; Richard, Duke of Gloucester; and from
this time the two boys were almost always designated by these names.

Suitable persons, too, were appointed to take
charge of the boys, for the purpose of conduct-
ing their education, and also to manage their
estates until they should become of age.

There have been a great many disputes in respect to Richard's appearance and character at
this time. For a long period after his death,
people generally believed that he was, from his
very childhood, an ugly little monster, that nobody could look upon without fear; and, in
fact, he was very repulsive in his personal appearance when he grew up, but at this time of
his life the historians and biographers who saw
and knew him say that he was quite a pretty

boy, though puny and weak. His face was
handsome enough, though his form was frail,
and not perfectly symmetrical. Those who had
charge of him tried to strengthen his constitution by training him to the martial exercises
and usages which were practiced in those days,
and especially by accustoming him to wear the
ponderous armor which was then in use.

This armor was made of iron or steel. It
consisted of a great number of separate pieces,
which, when they were all put on, incased almost the whole body, so as to defend it against
blows coming from any quarter. First, there
was the helmet, or cap of steel, with large oval
pieces coming down to protect the ears. Next
came the *gorget*, as it was called, which was a
sort of collar to cover the neck. Then there
were elbow pieces to guard the elbows, and
shoulder-plates for the shoulders, and a breast-
plate or buckler for the front, and greaves for
the legs and thighs. These things were necessary in those days, or at least they were advan-
tageous, for they afforded pretty effectual protection against all the ordinary weapons which
were then in use. But they made the warriors
themselves so heavy and unwieldy as very
greatly to interfere with the freedom of their
movements when engaged in battle. There

was, indeed, a certain advantage in this weight, as it made the shock with which the knight on horseback encountered his enemy in the charge so much the more heavy and overpowering; but if he were by any accident to lose his seat and fall to the ground, he was generally so encumbered by his armor that he could only partially raise himself therefrom. He was thus compelled to lie almost helpless until his enemy came to kill him, or his squire or some other friend came to help him up.*

Of course, to be able to manage one's self at all in these habiliments of iron and steel, there was required not only native strength of constitution, but long and careful training, and it was a very important part of the education of young men of rank in Richard's days to familiarize them with the use of this armor, and inure them to the weight of it. Suits of it were made for boys, the size and weight of each suit being fitted to the form and strength of the wearer. Many of these suits of boys' armor are still preserved in England. There are several specimens to be seen in the Tower of London. They are in the apartment called the Horse Armory, which is a vast hall with effigies of horses, and of men mounted upon them,

* See engraving on page 148.

all completely armed with the veritable suits
of steel which the men and the horses that they
represent actually wore when they were alive.
The horses are arranged along the sides of the
room in regular order from the earliest ages
down to the time when steel armor of this kind
ceased to be worn.

These suits of armor were very costly, and
the boys for whom they were made were, of
course, filled with feelings of exultation and
pride when they put them on; and, heavy and
uncomfortable as such clothing must have been,
they were willing to wear it, and to practice the
required exercises in it. When actually made
of steel, the armor was very expensive, and such
could only be afforded for young princes and
nobles of very high rank; for other young
men, various substitutes were provided; but all
were trained, either in the use of actual armor,
or of substitutes, to perform a great number
and variety of exercises. They were taught,
when they were old enough, to spring upon a
horse with as much armor upon them and in
their hands as possible; to run races; to see how
long they could continue to strike heavy blows
in quick succession with a battle-axe or club,
as if they were beating an enemy lying upon
the ground, and trying to break his armor to

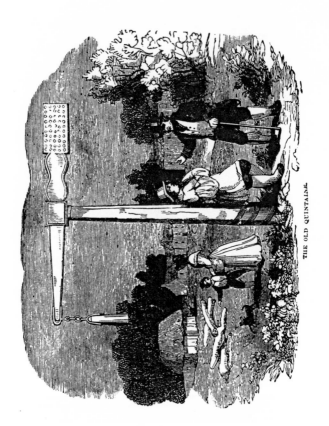

THE OLD QUINTAIN.

pieces; to dance and throw summersets; to
mount upon a horse behind another person by
leaping from the ground, and assisting themselves only by one hand, and other similar
things. One feat which they practiced was to
climb up between two partition walls built pretty near together, by bracing their back against
one wall, and working with their knees and
hands against the other. Another feat was to
climb up a ladder on the under side by means
of the hands alone.

Another famous exercise, or perhaps rather
game, was performed with what was called the
quintaine. The quintaine consisted of a stout
post set in the ground, and rising about ten or
twelve feet above the surface. Across the top
was a strong bar, which turned on a pivot made
in the top of the post, so that it would go round
and round. To one end of this cross-bar there
was fixed a square board for a target; to the
other end was hung a heavy club. The cross-
bar was so poised upon the central pivot that
it would move very easily. In playing the
game, the competitors, mounted on horseback,
were to ride, one after another, under the target-end of the cross-bar, and hurl their spears
at it with all their force. The blow from the
spear would knock the target-end of the cross-

bar away, and so bring round the other end, with its heavy club, to strike a blow on the horseman's head if he did not get instantly out of the way.   It was as if he were to strike one enemy in front in battle, while there was another enemy ready on the instant to strike him from behind.

There is one of these ancient quintaines now standing on the green in the village of Offham, in Kent.

Such exercises as these were, of course, only fitted for men, or at least for boys who had nearly attained to their full size and strength. There were other games and exercises intended for smaller boys.   There are many rude pictures in ancient books illustrating these old games.   In one they are playing ball; in another they are playing shuttle-cock.   The battle-doors that they use are very rude.

PLAYING BALL.

These pictures show how ancient these common games are.   In another picture the boys

Jumping through a hoop.   The two brothers companions

BATTLE-DOOR AND SHUTTLE-COCK.

are playing with a hoop. Two of them are holding the hoop up between them, and the third is preparing to jump through it, head foremost. His plan is to come down on the other side upon his hands, and so turn a summerset, and come up on his feet beyond.

In these exercises and amusements, and, indeed, in all his occupations, Richard had his brother George, the Duke of Clarence, for his playmate and companion. George was not only older than Richard, but he was also much more healthy and athletic; and some persons have thought that Richard injured himself, and perhaps, in some degree, increased the deformity which he seems to have suffered from in later years, or perhaps brought it on entirely, by

overloading himself, in his attempts to keep
pace with his brother in these exercises, with
burdens of armor, or by straining himself in
athletic exertions which were beyond his powers.

The intellectual education of the boys was
not entirely neglected. They learned to read
and write, though they could not write much,
or very well. Their names are still found, as
they signed them to ancient documents, several
of which remain to the present day. The following is a fac-simile of Richard's signature,
copied exactly from one of those documents.

RICHARD'S SIGNATURE.

Richard continued in this state of pupilage
in some of the castles belonging to the family
from the time that his brother began to reign
until he was about fourteen years of age. Edward, the king, was then twenty-four, and Clarence about seventeen.

CHAPTER V.

WARWICK, THE KING-MAKER.

RICHARD'S brother, Edward the Fourth, began to reign when Richard was about eight or nine years of age. His reign continued—with a brief interruption, which will be hereafter explained—for twenty years; so that, for a very important period of his life, after he arrived at some degree of maturity, namely, from the time that he was fourteen to the time that he was thirty, Richard was one of his brother's subjects. He was a prince, it is true, and a prince of the very highest rank—the next person but one, in fact, in the line of succession to the crown. His brother George, the Duke of Clarence, of course, being older than he, came before him; but both the young men, though princes, were subjects. They were under their brother Edward's authority, and bound to serve and obey him as their rightful sovereign; next to him, however, they were the highest personages in the realm. George was, from this time, generally called Clarence, and Richard, Gloucester.

. The reader may perhaps feel some interest and curiosity in learning what became of Queen Margaret and old King Henry after they were driven out of the country toward the north, at the time of Edward's. accession. Their prospects seemed, at the time, to be hopelessly ruined, but their case was destined to furnish another very striking instance of the extraordinary reverses of fortune which marked the history of nearly all the great families during the whole course of this York and Lancaster quarrel. In about ten years from the time when Henry and Margaret were driven away, apparently into hopeless exile, they came back in triumph, and were restored to power, and Edward himself, in his turn, was ignominiously expelled from the kingdom. The narrative of the circumstances through which these events were brought about forms quite a romantic story.

In order, however, that this story may be more clearly understood, I will first enumerate the principal personages that take a part in it, and briefly remind the reader of the position which they respectively occupied, and the relations which they sustained to each other.

First, there is the family of King Henry, consisting of himself and his wife, Queen Margaret, and his little son Edward, who had received the title of Prince of Wales. This boy was about eight years old at the time his father and mother were driven away. We left them, in the last chapter, flying toward the frontiers of Scotland to save their lives, leaving to Edward and his troops the full possession of the kingdom.

Henry and his little son, the Prince of Wales, of course represent the house of Lancaster in the dispute for the succession.

The house of York was represented by Edward, whose title, as king, was Edward the Fourth, and his two brothers, George and Richard, or, as they were now generally called, Clarence and Gloucester. In case Edward should be married and have a son, his son would succeed him, and George and Richard would be excluded; if, however, he should die without issue, then George would become king; and if George should die without issue, and Richard should survive him, then Richard would succeed. Thus, as matters now stood, George and Richard were presumptive heirs to the crown, and it was natural that they should wish that their brother Edward should never be married.

Besides these two brothers, who were the only ones of all his brothers that were now living, Edward had a sister named Margaret. Margaret was four years younger than Edward the king, and about six years older than Richard. She was now about seventeen. A young lady of that age in the family of a king in those days was quite a treasure, as the king was enabled to promote his political schemes sometimes very effectually by bestowing her in marriage upon this great prince or that, as would best further the interests which he had in view in foreign courts.

This young lady, Edward's sister, being of the same name—Margaret—with the queen of old King Henry, was distinguished from her by being called Margaret of York, as she belonged to the York family. The queen was generally known as Margaret of Anjou. Anjou was the place of her nativity.

The next great personage to be named is the Earl of Warwick. He was the man, as you will doubtless recollect, who was in command of the sea between England and the Continent at the time when Lady Cecily wished to send her children, George and Richard, away after their father's death, and who assisted in arranging their flight. He was a man of great power and influence, and of such an age and character that he exerted a vast ascendency over all within his influence. Without him, Edward never would have conquered the Lancaster

party, and he knew very well that if Warwick,
and all those whom Warwick would carry with
him, were to desert him, he should not be able
to retain his kingdom. Indeed, Warwick received the surname of *King-maker* from the
fact that, in repeated instances during this quarrel, he put down one dynasty and raised up the
other, just as he pleased. He belonged to a
great and powerful family named Neville. As
soon as Edward was established on his throne,
Warwick, almost as a matter of course, became
prime minister. One of his brothers was made
chancellor, and a great number of other posts
of distinction and honor were distributed among
the members of the Neville family. Indeed, although Edward was nominally king, it might
have been considered in some degree a question
whether it was the house of York or the house
of Neville that actually reigned in England.

The Earl of Warwick had two daughters.
Their names were Isabella and Anne. These
two young ladies the earl reckoned, as Edward did his sister Margaret, among the most
important of his political resources. By marrying them to persons of very high position,
he could strengthen his alliances and increase
his power. There was even a possibility, he
thought, of marrying one of them to the King

of England, or to a prince who would become king.

Thus we have for the three great parties to the transactions now to be described, first, the representatives of the house of Lancaster, the feeble Henry, the energetic and strong-minded Margaret of Anjou, and their little son, the Prince of Wales; secondly, the representatives of the house of York, King Edward the Fourth, the two young men his brothers, George, Duke of Clarence, and Richard, Duke of Gloucester, and his sister Margaret; and, thirdly, between these two parties, as it were, the Earl of Warwick and his two daughters, Isabella and Anne, standing at the head of a vast family influence, which ramified to every part of the kingdom, and was powerful enough to give the ascendency to either side, in favor of which they might declare.

We are now prepared to follow Queen Margaret in her flight toward the north with her husband and her son, at the time when Edward the Fourth overcame her armies and ascended the throne. She pressed on as rapidly as possible, taking the king and the little prince with her, and accompanied and assisted in her flight by a few attendants, till she had crossed the frontier and was safe in Scotland. The Scots

espoused her cause, and assisted her to raise
fresh troops, with which she made one or two
short incursions into England; but she soon
found that she could do nothing effectual in
this way, and so, after wasting some time in
fruitless attempts, she left Scotland with the
king and the prince, and went to France.

Here she entered into negotiations with the
King of France, and with other princes and po-
tentates on the Continent, with a view of raising men and money for a new invasion of England. At first these powers declined to assist
her. They said that their treasuries were exhausted, and that they had no men. At last,
however, Margaret promised to the King of
France that if he would furnish her with a fleet
and an army, by which she could recover the
kingdom of her husband, she would cede to him
the town of Calais, which, though situated on
the coast of France, was at that time an English
possession. This was a very tempting offer,
for Calais was a fortress of the first class, and a
military post either for England or France of a
very important character.

The king consented to this proposal. He
equipped a fleet and raised an army, and Margaret set sail for England, taking the king and
the prince with her. Her plan was to land in

the northern part of the island, near the frontiers of Scotland, where she expected to find the
country more friendly to the Lancastrian line
than the people were toward the south. As
soon as she landed she was joined by many of
the people, and she succeeded in capturing some
castles and small towns. But the Earl of Warwick, who was, as has been already said, the
prime minister under Edward, immediately
raised an army of twenty thousand men, and
marched to the northward to meet her. Margaret's French army was wholly unprepared to
encounter such a force as this, so they fled to
their ships. All but about five hundred of the
men succeeded in reaching the ships. The five
hundred were cut to pieces. Margaret herself
was detained in making arrangements for the
king and the prince. She concluded not to
take them to sea again, but to send them secretly into Wales, while she herself went back to
France to see if she could not procure re-enforcements. She barely had time, at last, to
reach the ships herself, so close at hand were
her enemies. As soon as the queen had embarked, the fleet set sail. The queen had saved
nearly all the money and all the stores which
she had brought with her from France, and she
hoped still to preserve them for another at-

tempt. But the fleet had scarcely got off from the shore when a terrible storm arose, and the ships were all driven upon the rocks and dashed to pieces. The money and the stores were all lost; a large portion of the men were drowned; Margaret herself and the captain of the fleet saved themselves, and, as soon as the storm was over, they succeeded in making their escape back to Berwick in an old fishing-boat which they obtained on the shore.

Soon after this, Margaret, with the captain of the fleet and a very small number of faithful followers who still adhered to her, sailed back again to France.

The disturbances, however, which her landing had occasioned, did not cease immediately on her departure. The Lancastrian party all over England were excited and moved to action by the news of her coming, and for two years insurrections were continually taking place, and many battles were fought, and great numbers of people were killed. King Henry was all this time kept in close concealment, sometimes in Wales, and sometimes among the lakes and mountains in Westmoreland. He was conveyed from place to place by his adherents in the most secret manner, the knowledge in respect to his situation being confined

9—7

to the smallest possible number of persons. This continued for two or three years. At last, however, while the friends of the king were attempting secretly to convey him to a certain castle in Yorkshire, he was seen and recognized by one of his enemies. A plan was immediately formed to make him prisoner. The plan succeeded. The king was surprised by an overwhelming force, which broke into the castle and seized him while he sat at dinner. His captors, and those who were lying in wait to assist them, galloped off at once with their prisoner to London. King Edward shut him up in the Tower, and he remained there, closely confined and strongly guarded, for a long time.

Thus King Henry's life was saved, but of those who espoused his cause, and made attempts to restore him, great numbers were seized and beheaded in the most cruel manner. It was Edward's policy to slay all the leaders. It was said that after a battle he would ride with a company of men over the ground, and kill every wounded or exhausted man of rank that still remained alive, though he would spare the common soldiers. Sometimes, when he got men that were specially obnoxious to him into his hands, he would put them to death in the most cruel and ignominious manner. One dis-

tinguished knight, that had been taken prisoner
by Warwick, was brought to King Edward,
who, at that time, as it happened, was sick, and
by Edward's orders was treated most brutally.
He was first taken out into a public place, and
his spurs were struck off from his feet by a
cook. This was one of the greatest indignities
that a knight could suffer. Then his coat of
arms was torn off from him, and another coat,
inside out, was put upon him. Then he was
made to walk barefoot to the end of the town,
and there was laid down upon his back on a
sort of drag, and so drawn to the place of execution, where his head was cut off on a block
with a broad-axe.

Such facts as these show what a state of ex-
asperation the two great parties of York and
Lancaster were in toward each other throughout the kingdom. It is necessary to understand this, in order fully to appreciate the im-
port and consequences of the very extraordinary transaction which is now to be related.

It seems there was a certain knight named
Sir John Gray, a Lancastrian, who had been
killed at one of the great battles which had
been fought during the war. He had also been
attainted, as it was called—that is, sentence had
been pronounced against him on a charge of

7

high treason, by which his estates were forfeited, and his wife and children, of course, reduced to poverty. The name of his wife was
Elizabeth Woodville. She was the daughter
of a noble knight named Sir Richard Woodville. Her mother's name was Jacquetta. On
the death and attainder of her husband, being
reduced to great poverty and distress, she went
home to the house of her father and mother, at
a beautiful manor which they possessed at Graf-
ton. She was quite young, and very beautiful.

It happened that by some means or other
Edward paid a visit one day to the Lady Jacquetta, at her manor, as he was passing through
the country. Whether this visit was accidental, or whether it was contrived by Jacquetta,
does not appear. However this may be, the
beautiful widow came into the presence of the
king, and, throwing herself at his feet, begged
and implored him to revoke the attainder of
her husband for the sake of her innocent and
helpless children. The king was much moved
by her beauty and by her distress. From pity-
ing her he soon began to love her. And yet
it seemed impossible that he should marry her.
Her rank, in the first place, was far below his,
and then, what was worse, she belonged to the
Lancastrian party, the king's implacable ene-

mies. The king knew very well that all his own partisans would be made furious at the idea of such a match, and that, if they knew that it was in contemplation, they would resist it to the utmost of their power. For a time he did not know what he should do. At length, however, his love for the beautiful widow, as might easily be foreseen, triumphed over all considerations of prudence, and he was secretly married to her. The marriage took place in the morning, in a very private manner, in the month of May, in 1464.

The king kept the marriage secret nearly all summer. He thought it best to break the subject to his lords and nobles gradually, as he had opportunity to communicate it to them one by one. In this way it at length became known, without producing, at any one time, any special sensation, and toward the fall preparations were made for openly acknowledging the union.

Although the knowledge of the king's marriage produced no sudden outbreak of opposition, it awakened a great deal of secret indignation and rage, and gave occasion to many suppressed mutterings and curses. Of course, every leading family of the realm, that had been on Edward's side in the civil wars, which con-

Ancient portrait of Edward IV.

KING EDWARD IV.

This engraving is a portrait of King Edward as he appeared at this time. It is copied from an ancient painting,
and doubtless represents correctly the character and expression of his countenance, and one form, at least, of dress which
he was accustomed to wear. He was, at the time of his
marriage, about twenty-two years of age. Elizabeth was
ten years older.

Portrait of Queen Elizabeth Woodville.

QUEEN ELIZABETH WOODVILLE.

This engraving represents the queen. It is taken, like the other, from an ancient portrait, and no doubt corresponds closely to the original.

tained a marriageable daughter, had been forming hopes and laying plans to secure this magnificent match for themselves. Those who had

no marriageable daughters of their own joined their nearest relatives and friends in their
schemes, or formed plans for some foreign alliance with a princess of France, or Burgundy,
or Holland, whichever would best harmonize
with the political schemes that they wished to
promote. The Earl of Warwick seems to have
belonged to the former class. He had two
daughters, as has already been stated. It would
very naturally be his desire that the king, if he
were to take for his wife any English subject
at all, should make choice of one of these. Of
course, he was more than all the rest irritated
and vexed at what the king had done. He
communicated his feelings to Clarence, but concealed them from the king. Clarence was, of
course, ready to sympathize with the earl. He
was ready enough to take offense at any thing
connected with the king's marriage on very
slight grounds, for it was very much for his interest, as the next heir, that his brother should
not be married at all.

The earl and Clarence, however, thought it
best for the time to suppress and conceal their
opposition to the marriage; so they joined very
readily in the ceremonies connected with the
public acknowledgment of the queen. A vast
assemblage of nobles, prelates, and other grand

WESTMINSTER IN TIMES OF PUBLIC CELEBRATIONS.

dignitaries was convened, and Elizabeth was brought forward before them and formally presented. The Earl of Warwick and Clarence appeared in the foremost rank among her friends on this occasion. They took her by the hand, and, leading her forward, presented her to the assembled multitude of lords and ladies, who welcomed her with long and loud acclamations.

Soon after this a grand council was convened, and a handsome income was settled upon the queen, to enable her properly to maintain the dignity of her station.

Early in the next year preparations were made for a grand coronation of the queen. Foreign princes were invited to attend the ceremony, and many came, accompanied by large bodies of knights and squires, to do honor to the occasion. The coronation took place in May. The queen was conveyed in procession through the streets of London on a sort of open palanquin, borne by horses most magnificently caparisoned. Vast crowds of people assembled along the streets to look at the procession as it passed. The next day the coronation itself took place in Westminster, and it was followed by games, feasts, tournaments, and public rejoicings of every kind, which lasted many days.

Thus far every thing on the surface, at least, had gone well; but it was not long after the coronation before the troubles which were to be expected from such a match began to develop themselves in great force. The new queen was ambitious, and she was naturally desirous of bringing her friends forward into places of influence and honor. The king was, of course, ready to listen to her recommendations; but then all her friends were Lancastrians. They were willing enough, it is true, to change their politics and to become Yorkists for the sake of the rewards and honors which they could obtain by the change, but the old friends of the king were greatly exasperated to find the important posts, one after another, taken away from them, and given to their hated enemies.

Then, besides the quarrel for the political offices, there were a great many of the cherished matrimonial plans and schemes of the old families interfered with and broken up by the queen's family thus coming into power. It happened that the queen had five unmarried sisters. She began to form plans for securing for them men of the highest rank and position in the realm. This, of course, thwarted the plans and disappointed the hopes of all those families who had been scheming to gain these

WARWICK IN THE PRESENCE OF THE FRENCH KING.

husbands for their own daughters. To see five
great heirs of dukes and barons thus withdrawn
from the matrimonial market, and employed to
increase the power and prestige of their ancient
and implacable foes, filled the souls of the old
Yorkist families with indignation. Parties were
formed. The queen and her family and friends
—the Woodvilles and Grays—with all their adherents, were on one side; the Neville family,
with the Earl of Warwick at their head, and
most of the old Yorkist noblemen, were on the
other; Clarence joined the Earl of Warwick;
Richard, on the other hand, or Gloucester, as
he was now called, adhered to the king.

Things went on pretty much in this way for
two years. There was no open quarrel, though
there was a vast deal of secret animosity and
bickering. The great world at court was divided into two sets, or cliques, that hated each
other very cordially, though both, for the present, pretended to support King Edward as the
rightful sovereign of the country. The struggle was for the honors and offices under him.
The families who still adhered to the old Lancastrian party, and to the rights of Henry and
of the little Prince of Wales, withdrew, of course,
altogether from the court, and, retiring to their
castles, brooded moodily there over their fallen

fortunes, and waited in expectation of better times. Henry was imprisoned in the Tower; Margaret and the Prince of Wales were on the Continent. They and their friends were, of course, watching the progress of the quarrel between the party of the Earl of Warwick and that of the king, hoping that it might at last lead to an open rupture, in which case the Lancastrians might hope for Warwick's aid to bring them again into power.

And now another circumstance occurred which widened this breach very much indeed. It arose from a difference of opinion between King Edward and the Earl of Warwick in respect to the marriage of the king's sister Margaret, known, as has already been said, as Margaret of York. There was upon the Continent a certain Count Charles, the son and heir of the Duke of Burgundy, who demanded her hand. The count's family had been enemies of the house of York, and had done every thing in their power to promote Queen Margaret's plans, so long as there was any hope for her; but when they found that King Edward was firmly established on the throne, they came over to his side, and now the count demanded the hand of the Princess Margaret in marriage; but the stern old Earl of Warwick did not like such friendship as this, so he recommended that the count should be refused, and that Margaret should have for her husband one of the princes of France.

Now King Edward himself preferred Count Charles for the husband of Margaret, and this chiefly because the queen, his wife, preferred him on account of the old friendship which had subsisted between his family and the Lancastrians. Besides this, however, Flanders, the country over which the count was to reign on the death of his father, was at that time so situated that an alliance with it would be of greater advantage to Edward's political plans than an alliance with France. But, notwithstanding this, the earl was so earnest in urging his opinion, that finally Edward yielded, and the earl was dispatched to France to negotiate the marriage with the French prince.

The earl set off on this embassy in great magnificence. He landed in Normandy with a vast train of attendants, and proceeded in almost royal state toward Paris. The King of France, to honor his coming and the occasion, came forth to meet him. The meeting took place at Rouen. The proposals were well received by the French king. The negotiations were continued for eight or ten days, and at last every

9—8

thing was arranged. For the final closing of the contract, it was necessary that a messenger from the King of France should proceed to London. The king appointed an archbishop and some other dignitaries to perform the service. The earl then returned to England, and was soon followed by the French embassadors, expecting that every thing essential was settled, and that nothing but a few formalities remained.

But, in the mean time, while all this had been going on in France, Count Charles had quietly sent an embassador to England to press his claim to the princess's hand. This messenger managed this business very skillfully, so as not to attract any public attention to what he was doing; and besides, the earl being away, the queen, Elizabeth, could exert all her influence over her husband's mind unimpeded. Edward was finally persuaded to promise Margaret's hand to the count, and the contracts were made; so that, when the earl and the French embassadors arrived, they found, to their astonishment and dismay, that a rival and enemy had stepped in during their absence and secured the prize.

The Earl of Warwick was furious when he learned how he had been deceived. He had been insulted, he said, and disgraced. Edward

made no attempt to pacify him; indeed, any
attempt that he could have made would probably have been fruitless. The earl withdrew
from the court, went off to one of his castles,
and shut himself up there in great displeasure.

The quarrel now began to assume a very serious air. Edward suspected that the earl was
forming plots and conspiracies against him.
He feared that he was secretly designing to
take measures for restoring the Lancastrian line
to the throne. He was alarmed for his personal
safety. He expelled all Warwick's family and
friends from the court, and, whenever he went
out in public, he took care to be always attended by a strong body-guard, as if he thought
there was danger of an attempt upon his life.

At length one of the earl's brothers, the
youngest of the family, who was at that time
Archbishop of York, interposed to effect a reconciliation. We have not space here to give a
full account of the negotiations; but the result
was, a sort of temporary peace was made, by
which the earl again returned to court, and was
restored apparently to his former position. But
there was no cordial good-will between him and
the king. Edward dreaded the earl's power,
and hated the stern severity of his character,
while the earl, by the commanding influence

8

which he exerted in the realm, was continually
thwarting both Edward and Elizabeth in their
plans.

Edward and Elizabeth had now been married some time, but they had no son, and, of
course, no heir, for daughters in those days did
not inherit the English crown. Of course, Clarence, Edward's second brother, was the next
heir. This increased the jealousy which the
two brothers felt toward each other, and tended
very much to drive Clarence away from Edward, and to increase the intimacy between Clarence and Warwick. At length, in 1468, it was
announced that a marri. ge was in contemplation between Clarence and Isabella, the Earl
of Warwick's oldest daughter. Edward and
Queen Elizabeth were very much displeased
and very much alarmed when they heard of
this plan. If carried into effect, it would bind
Clarence and the Warwick influence together
in indissoluble bonds, and make their power
much more formidable than ever before. Every body would say when the marriage was
concluded,

"Now, in case Edward should die, which
event may happen at any time, the earl's daughter will be queen, and then the earl will have a
greater influence than ever in the disposition

of offices and honors. It behooves us, therefore, to make friends with him in season, so as
to secure his good-will in advance, before he
comes into power."

King Edward and his queen, seeing how much
this match was likely at once to increase the
earl's importance, did every thing in their power to prevent it. But they could not succeed.
The earl was determined that Clarence and his
daughter should be married. The opposition
was, however, so strong at court that the marriage could not be celebrated at London; so
the ceremony was performed at Calais, which
city was at that time under the earl's special
command. The king and queen remained at
London, and made no attempt to conceal their
vexation and chagrin.

CHAPTER VI.

THE DOWNFALL OF YORK.

EDWARD'S apprehension and anxiety in respect to the danger that Warwick might be concocting schemes to restore the Lancastrian line to the throne were greatly increased by the sudden breaking out of insurrections in the northern part of the island, while Warwick and Clarence were absent in Calais, on the occasion of Clarence's marriage to Isabella. The insurgents did not demand the restoration of the Lancastrian line, but only the removal of the queen's family and relations from the council. The king raised an armed force, and marched to the northward to meet the rebels. But his army was disaffected, and he could do nothing. They fled before the advancing army of insurgents, and Edward went with them to Nottingham Castle, where he shut himself up, and wrote urgently to Warwick and Clarence to come to his aid.

Warwick made no haste to obey this command. After some delay, however, he left Calais in command of one of his lieutenants and

repaired to Nottingham, where he soon released
the king from his dangerous situation. He
quelled the rebellion too, but not until the insurgents had seized the father and one of the
brothers of the queen, and cut off their heads.

In the mean time, the Lancastrians themselves, thinking that this was a favorable time
for them, began to put themselves in motion.
Warwick was the only person who was capable
of meeting them and putting them down. This
he did, taking the king with him in his train,
in a condition more like that of a prisoner than
a sovereign. At length, however, the rebellions were suppressed, and all parties returned
to London.

There now took place what purported to be
a grand reconciliation. Treaties were drawn
up and signed between Warwick and Clarence
on one side, and the king on the other, by which
both parties bound themselves to forgive and
forget all that had passed, and thenceforth to
be good friends; but, notwithstanding all the
solemn signings and sealings with which these
covenants were secured, the actual condition of
the parties in respect to each other remained
entirely unchanged, and neither of the three
felt a whit more confidence in the others after
the execution of these treaties than before.

At last the secret distrust which they felt toward each other broke out openly. Warwick's brother, the Archbishop of York, made an entertainment at one of his manors for a party of guests, in which were included the king, the Duke of Clarence, and the Earl of Warwick. It was about three months after the treaties were signed that this entertainment was made, and the feast was intended to celebrate and cement the good understanding which it was now agreed was henceforth to prevail. The king arrived at the manor, and, while he was in his room making his toilet for the supper, which was all ready to be served, an attendant came to him and whispered in his ear,

"Your majesty is in danger. There is a band of armed men in ambush near the house."

The king was greatly alarmed at hearing this. He immediately stole out of the house, mounted his horse, and, with two or three followers, rode away as fast as he could ride. He continued his journey all night, and in the morning arrived at Windsor Castle.

Then followed new negotiations between Warwick and the king, with mutual reproaches, criminations, and recriminations without number. Edward insisted that treachery was intended at the house to which he had been in-

vited, and that he had barely escaped, by his
sudden flight, from falling into the snare. But
Warwick and his friends denied this entirely,
and attributed the flight of the king to a wholly unreasonable alarm, caused by his jealous
and suspicious temper. At last Edward suffered himself to be reassured, and then came
new treaties and a new reconciliation.

This peace was made in the fall of 1469,
and in the spring of 1470 a new insurrection
broke out. The king believed that Warwick
himself, and Clarence, were really at the bottom
of these disturbances, but still he was forced to
send them with bodies of troops to subdue the
rebels; he, however, immediately raised a large
army for himself, and proceeded to the seat of
war. He reached the spot before Warwick and
Clarence arrived there. He gave battle to the
insurgents, and defeated them. He took a great
many prisoners, and beheaded them. He found,
or pretended to find, proof that Warwick and
Clarence, instead of intending to fight the insurgents, had made their arrangements for joining them on the following day, and that he
had been just in time to defeat their treachery.
Whether he really found evidence of these intentions on the part of Warwick and Clarence
or not, or whether he was flushed by the ex-

Warwick comes to open war with the king.

citement of victory, and resolved to seize the
occasion to cut loose at once and forever from
the entanglement in which he had been bound,
is somewhat uncertain. At all events, he now
declared open war against Warwick and Clarence, and set off immediately on his march to
meet them, at the head of a force much superi-
or to theirs.

Warwick and Clarence marched and coun-
termarched, and made many manœuvres to escape a battle, and during all this time their
strength was rapidly diminishing. As long as
they were nominally on the king's side, however really hostile to him, they had plenty of
followers; but, now that they were in open war
against him, their forces began to melt away.
In this emergency, Warwick suddenly changed
all his plans. He disbanded his army, and then
taking all his family with him, including Clarence and Isabella, and accompanied by an in-
considerable number of faithful friends, he
marched at the head of a small force which he
retained as an escort to the sea-port of Dart-
mouth, and then embarked for Calais.

The vessels employed to transport the party
formed quite a little fleet, so numerous were the
servants and attendants that accompanied the
fugitives. They embarked without delay on

reaching the coast, as they were in haste to make the passage and arrive at Calais, for Isabella, Clarence's wife, was about to become a mother, and at Calais they thought that they should all be, as it were, at home.

It will be remembered that the Earl of Warwick was the governor of Calais, and that when he left it he had appointed a lieutenant to take command of it during his absence. Before his ship arrived off the port this lieutenant had received dispatches from Edward, which had been hurried to him by a special messenger, informing him that Warwick was in rebellion against his sovereign, and forbidding the lieutenant to allow him or his party to enter the town.

Accordingly, when Warwick's fleet arrived off the port, they found the guns of the batteries pointed at them, and sentinels on the piers warning them not to attempt to land.

Warwick was thunderstruck.   To be thus refused admission to his own fortress by his own lieutenant was something amazing, as well as outrageous.   The earl was at first completely bewildered; but, on demanding an explanation, the lieutenant sent him word that the refusal to land was owing to the people of the town.   They, he said, having learned that he and the king had come to open war, insisted

that the fortress should be reserved for their
sovereign. Warwick then explained the situation that his daughter was in; but the lieutenant was firm. The determination of the people was so strong, he said, that he could not
control it. Finally, the child was born on board
the ship, as it lay at anchor off the port, and all
the aid or comfort which the party could get
from the shore consisted of two flagons of wine,
which the lieutenant, with great hesitation and
reluctance, allowed to be sent on board. The
child was a son. His birth was an event of
great importance, for he was, of course, as Clarence's son, a prince in the direct line of succession to the English crown.

At length, finding that he could not land at
Calais, Warwick sailed away with his fleet along
the coast of France till he reached the French
port of Harfleur. Here his ships were admit-
ted, and the whole party were allowed to land.

Then followed various intrigues, manœuvres,
and arrangements, which we have not time here
fully to unravel; but the end of all was, that in
a few weeks after the Earl of Warwick's landing in France, he repaired to a castle where
Margaret of Anjou and her son, the Prince of
Wales, were residing, and there, in the course
of a short time, he made arrangements to es-

pouse her cause, and assist in restoring her husband to the English throne, on condition that her son, the Prince of Wales, should marry his second daughter Anne. It is said that Queen Margaret for a long time refused to consent to this arrangement. She was extremely unwilling that her son, the heir to the English crown, should take for a wife the daughter of the hated enemy to whom the downfall of her family, and all the terrible calamities which had befallen them, had been mainly owing. She was, however, at length induced to yield. Her ambition gained the victory over her hate, and she consented to the alliance on a solemn oath being taken by Warwick that thenceforth he would be on her side, and do all in his power to restore her family to the throne.

This arrangement was accordingly carried into effect, and thus the earl had one of his daughters married to the next heir to the English crown in the line of York, and the other to the next heir in the line of Lancaster. He had now only to choose to which dynasty he would secure the throne. Of course, the oath which he had taken, like other political oaths taken in those days, was only to be kept so long as he should deem it for his interest to keep it.

He could not at once openly declare in favor

of King Henry, for fear of alienating Clarence
from him. But Clarence was soon drawn away.
King Edward, when he heard of the marriage
of Warwick's daughter with the Prince of
Wales, immediately formed a plan for sending
a messenger to negotiate with Clarence. He
could not do this openly, for he knew very well
that Warwick would not allow any avowed
messenger from Edward to land; so he sent a
lady. The lady was a particular friend of Isabella, Clarence's wife. She traveled privately
by the way of Calais. On the way she said
nothing about the object of her journey, but
gave out simply that she was going to join her
mistress, the Princess Isabella. On her arrival
she managed the affair with great discretion.
She easily obtained private interviews with
Clarence, and represented to him that Warwick,
now that his daughter was married to the heir
on the Lancastrian side, would undoubtedly lay
all his plans forthwith for putting that family
on the throne, and that thus Clarence would
lose all.

"And therefore," said she, "how much better it will be for you to leave him and return
to your brother Edward, who is ready to forgive and forget all the past, and receive you
again as his friend."

Clarence was convinced by these representa‧
tions, and soon afterward, watching his oppor‧
tunity, he made his way to England, and there
espoused his brother's cause, and was received
again into his service.

In the mean time, tidings were continually
coming to King Edward from his friends on
the Continent, warning him of Warwick's plans,
and bidding him to be upon his guard. But
Edward had no fear. He said he wished that
Warwick would come.

" All I ask of my friends on the other side
of the Channel," said he, " is that, when he does
come, they will not let him get away again be‧
fore I catch him—as he did before."

Edward's great friend across the Channel was
his brother-in-law, the Duke of Burgundy, the
same who, when Count Charles, had married
the Princess Margaret of York, as related in a
former chapter. The Duke of Burgundy pre‧
pared and equipped a fleet, and had it all in
readiness to intercept the earl in case he should
attempt to sail for England.

In the mean time, Queen Margaret and the
earl went on with their preparations. The
King of France furnished them with men, arms,
and money. When every thing was ready, the
earl sent word to the north of England, to some

of his friends and partisans there, to make a sort of false insurrection, in order to entice away Edward and his army from the capital. This plan succeeded. Edward heard of the rising, and, collecting all the troops which were at hand, he marched to the northward to put it down. Just at this time a sudden storm arose and dispersed the Duke of Burgundy's fleet. The earl then immediately put to sea, taking with him Margaret of Anjou and her son, the Prince of Wales, with his wife, the Earl of Warwick's daughter. The Prince of Wales was now about eighteen years old. The father, King Henry, Margaret's husband, was not joined with the party. He was all this time, as you will recollect, a prisoner in the Tower, where Warwick himself had shut him up when he deposed him in order to place Edward upon the throne.

All Europe looked on with astonishment at these proceedings, and watched the result with intense interest. Here was a man who, having, by a desperate and bloody war, deposed a king, and shut him up in prison, and compelled his queen and the prince his son, the heir, to fly from the country to save their lives, had now sought the exiles in their banishment, had married his own daughter to the prince, and was setting forth on an expedition for the purpose of liberating the father again, and restoring him to the throne.   The earl's fleet crossed the Channel safely, and landed on the coast of Devonshire, in the southwestern part of the island.   The landing of the expedition was the signal for great numbers of the nobles and high families throughout the realm to prepare for changing sides ; for it was the fact, throughout the whole course of these wars between the houses of York and Lancaster, that a large proportion of the nobility and gentry, and great numbers of other adventurers, who lived in various ways on the public, stood always ready at once to change sides whenever there was a prospect that another side was coming into power.   Then there were, in such a case as this, great numbers who were secretly in favor of the Lancaster line, but who were prevented from manifesting their preference while the house of York was in full possession of power.   All these persons were aroused and excited by the landing of Warwick.   King Edward found that his calls upon his friends to rally to his standard were not promptly obeyed.   His friends were beginning to feel some doubt whether it would be best to continue his friends.   A certain preacher in London had the courage to pray in public for

9—9

the "king in the Tower," and the manner in
which this allusion was received by the populace, and the excitement which it produced,
showed how ready the city of London was to
espouse Henry's cause.

These, and other such indications, alarmed
Edward very much. He turned to the southward again when he learned that Warwick had
landed. Richard, who had, during all this period, adhered faithfully to Edward's cause, was
with him, in command of a division of the army.
As Warwick himself was rapidly advancing toward the north at this time, the two armies soon
began to approach each other. As the time of
trial drew nigh, Edward found that his friends
and supporters were rapidly abandoning him.
At length, one day, while he was at dinner, a
messenger came in and told him that one of
the leading officers of the army, with the whole
division under his command, were waving their
caps and cheering for "King Harry." He saw
at once that all was lost, and he immediately
prepared to fly.

He was not far from the eastern coast at this
time, and there was a small vessel there under
his orders, which had been employed in bringing provisions from the Thames to supply his
army. There were also two Dutch vessels there.

The king took possession of these vessels, with
Richard, and the few other followers that went
with him, and put at once to sea. Nobody
knew where they were going.

Very soon after they had put to sea they
were attacked by pirates. They escaped only
by running their vessel on shore on the coast
of Finland. Here the king found himself in a
state of almost absolute destitution, so that he
had to pawn his clothing to satisfy the most
urgent demands. At length, after meeting with
various strange adventures, he found his way to
the Hague, where he was, for the time, in comparative safety.

As soon as Warwick ascertained that Edward had fled, he turned toward London, with
nothing now to impede his progress. He entered London in triumph. Clarence joined him,
and entered London in his train; for Clarence,
though he had gone to England with the intention of making common cause with his brother,
had not been able yet to decide positively
whether it would, on the whole, be for his interest to do so, and had, accordingly, kept himself in some degree uncommitted, and now he
turned at once again to Warwick's side.

The queen—Elizabeth Woodville—with her
mother Jacquetta, were residing at the Tower

at this time, where they had King Henry in their keeping; for the Tower was an extended group of buildings, in which palace and prison were combined in one. As soon as the queen learned that Edward was defeated, and that Warwick and Clarence were coming in triumph to London, she took her mother and three of her daughters—Elizabeth, Mary, and Cecily—who were with her at that time, and also a lady attendant, and hurried down the Tower stairs to a barge which was always in waiting there. She embarked on board the barge, and ordered the men to row her up to Westminster.

Westminster is at the upper end of London, as the Tower is at the lower. On arriving at Westminster, the whole party fled for refuge to a sanctuary there. This sanctuary was a portion of the sacred precincts of a church, from which a refugee could not be taken, according to the ideas of those times, without committing the dreadful crime of sacrilege. A part of the building remained standing for three hundred years after this time, as represented in the opposite engraving. It was a gloomy old edifice, and it must have been a cheerless residence for princesses and a queen.

In this sanctuary, the queen, away from her husband, and deprived of almost every comfort,

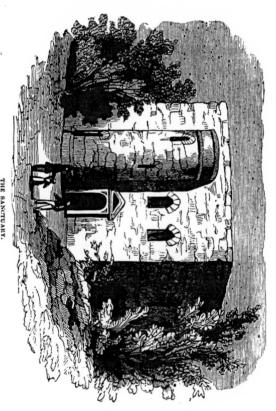

THE SANCTUARY.

gave birth to her first son. Some persons living near took compassion upon her forlorn and desolate condition, and rendered her such aid as was absolutely necessary, out of charity. The abbot of the monastery connected with the church sent in various conveniences, and a good woman named Mother Cobb, who lived near by, came in and acted as nurse for the mother and the child.

The child was baptized in the sanctuary a few days after he was born. He was named Edward, after his father. Of course, the birth of this son of King Edward cut off Clarence and his son from the succession on the York side. This little Edward was now the heir, and, about thirteen years after this, as we shall see in the sequel, he became King of England.

As soon as the Earl of Warwick reached London, he proceeded at once to the Tower to release old King Henry from his confinement. He found the poor king in a wretched plight. His apartment was gloomy and comfortless, his clothing was ragged, and his person squalid and dirty. The earl brought him forth from his prison, and, after causing his personal wants to be properly attended to, clothed him once more in royal robes, and conveyed him in state through London to the palace in Westminster, and established him there nominally as King of England, though Warwick was to all intents and purposes the real king. A Parliament was called, and all necessary laws were passed to sanction and confirm the dynasty. Queen Margaret, who, however, had not yet arrived from the Continent, was restored to her former rank, and the young Prince of Wales, now about eighteen years old, was the object of universal interest throughout the kingdom, as now the unquestioned and only heir to the crown.

CHAPTER VII.

THE DOWNFALL OF LANCASTER.

IT was in the month of October, 1470, that
old King Henry and his family were restored to the throne. Clarence, as we have
seen, being allied to Warwick by being married to his daughter, was induced to go over
with him to the Lancastrian side ; but Gloucester—that is, Richard—remained true to his own
line, and followed the fortunes of his brother,
in adverse as well as in prosperous times, with
unchanging fidelity. He was now with Edward in the dominions of the Duke of Burgundy, who, you will recollect, married Margaret,
Edward's sister, and who was now very naturally inclined to espouse Edward's cause.

The Duke of Burgundy did not, however,
dare to espouse Edward's cause too openly, for
fear of the King of France, who took the side
of Henry and Queen Margaret. He, however,
did all in his power secretly to befriend him.
Edward and Richard began immediately to
form schemes for going back to England and
recovering possession of the kingdom. The

Duke of Burgundy issued a public proclamation, in which it was forbidden that any of his subjects should join Edward, or that any expedition to promote his designs should be fitted out in any part of his dominions. This proclamation was for the sake of the King of France. At the same time that he issued these orders publicly, he secretly sent Edward a large sum of money, furnished him with a fleet of fifteen or twenty ships, and assisted him in collecting a force of twelve hundred men.

While he was making these arrangements and preparations on the Continent, Edward and his friends had also opened a secret communication with Clarence in England. It would, of course, very much weaken the cause of Edward and Richard to have Clarence against them; so Margaret, the wife of the Duke of Burgundy, interested herself in endeavoring to win him back again to their side. She had herself great influence over him, and she was assisted in her efforts by their mother, the Lady Cecily, who was still living in the neighborhood of London, and who was greatly grieved at Clarence's having turned against his brothers. The tie which bound Clarence to the Earl of Warwick was, of course, derived chiefly from his being married to Warwick's daughter. Warwick, how-

ever, did not trust wholly to this. As soon as
he had restored Henry to the throne, he contrived a cunning plan which he thought would
tend to bind Clarence still more strongly to
himself, and to alienate him completely from
Edward. This plan was to induce the Parliament to confiscate all Edward's estates and con-
fer them upon Clarence.

"Now," said Warwick to himself, when this
measure had been accomplished, "Clarence will
be sure to oppose Edward's return to England,
for he knows very well that if he should return
and be restored to the throne, he would, of
course, take all these estates back again."

But, while Edward was forming his plans on
the Continent for a fresh invasion of England,
Margaret sent messengers to Clarence, and their
persuasions, united to those of his mother, induced Clarence to change his mind. He was
governed by no principle whatever in what he
did, but only looked to see what would most
speedily and most fully gratify his ambition
and increase his wealth. So, when they argued
that it would be much better for him to be on
the side of his brothers, and assist in restoring
his own branch of the family to the throne, than
to continue his unnatural connection with Warwick and the house of Lancaster, he allowed

himself to be easily persuaded, and he promised that though, for the present, he should remain ostensibly a friend of Warwick, still, if
Edward and Richard would raise an expedition
and come to England, he would forsake Warwick and the Lancasters, and join them.

Accordingly, in the spring, when the fleet
and the forces were ready, Edward and Richard
set sail from the Low Country to cross the Channel. It was early in March. They intended
to proceed to the north of England and land
there. They had a very stormy passage, and
in the end the fleet was dispersed, and Edward
and Richard with great difficulty succeeded in
reaching the land. The two brothers were in
different ships, and they landed in different
places, a few miles apart from each other.
Their situation was now extremely critical, for
all England was in the power of Warwick and
the Lancastrians, and Edward and Richard were
almost entirely without men.

They, however, after a time, got together a
small force, consisting chiefly of the troops who
had come with them, and who had succeeded
at last in making their way to the land. At
the head of this force they advanced into the
country toward the city of York. Edward gave
out every where that he had not come with any

view of attempting to regain possession of the
throne, but only to recover his own private and
family estates, which had been unjustly confiscated, he said, and conferred upon his brother.
He acquiesced entirely, he said, in the restoration of Henry to the throne, and acknowledged.
him as king, and solemnly declared that he
would not do any thing to disturb the peace of
the country.

All this was treacherous and false; but Edward and Richard thought that they were not
yet strong enough to announce openly their
real designs, and, in the mean time, the uttering
of any false declarations which they might deem
it good policy to make was to be considered as
a stratagem justified by usage, as one of the legitimate resources of war.

So they went on, nobody opposing them.
They reached, at length, the city of York.
Here Edward met the mayor and aldermen of
the city, and renewed his declaration, which
he confirmed by a solemn oath, that he never
would lay any claim to the throne of England,
or do any thing to disturb King Henry in his
possession of it. He cried out, in a loud voice,
in the hearing of the people, " Long live King
Henry, and Prince Edward his son!" He wore
an ostrich feather, too, in his armor, which was

the badge of Prince Edward. The people of
York were satisfied with these protestations,
and allowed him to proceed.

His force was continually increasing as he
advanced, and at length, on crossing the River
Trent, he came to a part of the country where
almost the whole population had been on the
side of York during all the previous wars.
He began now to throw off his disguise, and to
avow more openly that his object was again to
obtain possession of the throne for the house of
York. His troops now began to exhibit the
white rose, which for many generations had
been the badge of the house of York, as the
red rose had been that of Lancaster.* In a
word, the country was every where aroused and
excited by the idea that another revolution was
impending, and all those whose ruling principle
it was to be always with the party that was uppermost began to make preparations for coming over to Edward's side.

In the mean time, however, Warwick, alarmed, had come from the northward to London to
meet the invaders at the head of a strong force.

---

* It was in consequence of this use of the roses, as the
badges of the two parties respectively, that the civil wars
between these two great families are often called in history
the Wars of the Roses.

Clarence was in command of one great division
of this force, and Warwick himself of the other.
The two bodies of troops marched at some little distance from each other. Edward shaped
his course so as to approach that commanded
by Clarence. Warwick did all he could to prevent this, being, apparently, somewhat suspicious that Clarence was not fully to be relied on.
But Edward succeeded, by dint of skillful manœuvring, in accomplishing his object, and thus
he and Clarence came into the neighborhood of
each other. The respective encampments were
only three miles apart. It seems, however, that
there were still some closing negotiations to be
made before Clarence was fully prepared to
take the momentous step that was now before
him. Richard was the agent of these negotiations. He went back and forth between the
two camps, conveying the proposals and coun-
ter-proposals from one party to the other, and
doing all in his power to remove obstacles from
the way, and to bring his brothers to an agreement. At last every thing was arranged. Clarence ordered his men to display the white rose
upon their armor, and then, with trumpets
sounding and banners flying, he marched forth
to meet Edward, and to submit himself to his
command.

When the column which he led arrived near
to Edward's camp, it halted, and Clarence himself, with a small body of attendants, advanced
to meet his brother ; Edward, at the same time,
leaving his encampment, in company with Richard and several noblemen, came forward too.
Thus Edward and Clarence met, as the old chron-
icle expresses it, "betwixt both hosts, where
was right kind and loving language betwixt
them two. And then, in like wise, spoke together the two Dukes of Clarence and Gloucester, and afterward the other noblemen that were
there with them; whereof all the people that
were there that loved them were right glad and
joyous, and thanked God highly for that joyous
meeting, unity and concord, hoping that there-
by should grow unto them prosperous fortune
in all that they should after that have to do."

Warwick was, of course, in a dreadful rage
when he learned that Clarence had betrayed
him and gone over to the enemy. He could
do nothing, however, to repair the mischief, and
he was altogether too weak to resist the two
armies now combined against him ; so he drew
back, leaving the way clear, and Edward, at the
head now of an overwhelming force, and accompanied by both his brothers, advanced directly to London.

He was received at the capital with great favor. Whoever was uppermost for the time being was always received with favor in England in those days, both in the capital and throughout the country at large. It was said, however, that the interest in Edward's fortunes, and in the succession of his branch of the family to the throne, was greatly increased at this time by the birth of his son, which had taken place in the sanctuary, as related in the last chapter, soon after Queen Elizabeth sought refuge there, at the time of Edward's expulsion from the kingdom. Of course, the first thing which Edward did after making his public entry into London was to proceed to the sanctuary to rejoin his wife, and deliver her from her duress, and also to see his new-born son.

Queen Margaret was out of the kingdom at this time, being on a visit to the Continent. She had her son, the Prince of Wales, with her; but Henry, the king, was in London. He, of course, fell into Edward's hands, and was immediately sent back a prisoner to the Tower.

Edward remained only a day or two in London, and then set off again, at the head of all his troops, to meet Warwick. He brought out King Henry from the Tower, and took him with the army as a prisoner.

9—10

Warwick had now strengthened himself so far that he was prepared for battle. The two armies approached each other not many miles from London. Before commencing hostilities, Clarence wished for an opportunity to attempt a reconciliation; he, of course, felt a strong desire to make peace, if possible, for his situation, in case of battle, would be painful in the extreme—his brothers on one side, and his father-in-law on the other, and he himself compelled to fight against the cause which he had abandoned and betrayed. So he sent a messenger to the earl, offering to act as mediator between him and his brother, in hopes of finding some mode of arranging the quarrel; but the earl, instead of accepting the mediation, sent back only invectives and defiance.

"Go tell your master," he said to the messenger, "that Warwick is not the man to follow the example of faithlessness and treason which the false, perjured Clarence has set him. Unlike him, I stand true to my oath, and this quarrel can only be settled by the sword."

Of course, nothing now remained but to fight the battle, and a most desperate and bloody battle it was. It was fought upon a plain at a place called Barnet. It lasted from four in the morning till ten.

DEATH OF WARWICK ON THE FIELD OF BARNET.

Richard came forward in the fight in a very conspicuous and prominent manner. He was now about eighteen years of age, and this was the first serious battle in which he had been actually engaged. He evinced a great deal of heroism, and won great praise by the ardor in which he rushed into the thickest of the fight, and by the manner in which he conducted himself there. The squires who attended him were both killed, but Richard himself remained unhurt.

In the end, Edward was victorious. The quarrel was thus decided by the sword, as Warwick had said, and decided, so far as the earl was concerned, terribly and irrevocably, for he himself was unhorsed upon the field, and slain. Many thousands of soldiers fell on each side, and great numbers of the leading nobles. The bodies were buried in one common trench, which was dug for the purpose on the plain, and a chapel was afterward erected over them, to mark and consecrate the spot.

It is said in respect to King Henry, who had been taken from the Tower and made to accompany the army to the field, that Edward placed him in the midst of the fight at Barnet, in the hope that he might in this way be slain, either by accident or design. This plan, how-

ever, if it were formed, did not succeed, for
Henry escaped unharmed, and, after the battle,
was taken back to London, and again conveyed
through the gloomy streets of the lower city to
his solitary prison in the Tower. The streets
were filled, after he had passed, with groups of
men of all ranks and stations, discussing the
strange and mournful vicissitudes in the life of
this hapless monarch, now for the second time
cut off from all his friends, and immured hopelessly in a dismal dungeon.

On the' very day of the battle of Barnet,
Queen Margaret, who had hastened her return
to England on hearing of Edward's invasion,
landed at Plymouth, in the southwestern part
of England. The young Prince of Wales, her
son, was with her. When she heard the terrible tidings of the loss of the battle of Barnet
and the death of Warwick, she was struck with
consternation, and immediately fled to an abbey in the neighborhood of the place where
she had landed, and took sanctuary there. She
soon, however, recovered from this panic, and
came forth again. She put herself, with her
son, at the head of the French troops which she
had brought with her, and collected also as
many more as she could induce to join her, and
then, marching slowly toward the northward,

STREET LEADING TO THE TOWER.

finally took a strong position on the River Severn, near the town of Tewkesbury. Tewkesbury is in the western part of England, near the frontiers of Wales.

Edward, having received intelligence of her movements, collected his forces also, and, accompanied by Clarence and Gloucester, went forth to meet her. The two armies met about three weeks after the battle of Barnet, in which Warwick was killed. All the flower of the English nobility were there, on one side or on the other.

Queen Margaret's son, the Prince of Wales, was now about eighteen years of age, and his mother placed him in command—nominally at the head of the army. Edward, on his side, assigned the same position to Richard, who was almost precisely of the same age with the Prince of Wales. Thus the great and terrible battle which ensued was fought, as it were, by two boys, cousins to each other, and neither of them out of their teens.

The operations were, however, really directed by older and more experienced men. The chief counselor on Margaret's side was the Duke of Somerset. Edward's army attempted, by means of certain evolutions, to entice the queen's army out of their camp. Somerset

wished to go, and he commanded the men to
follow. Some followed, but others remained
behind. Among those that remained behind
was a body of men under the command of a
certain Lord Wenlock. Somerset was angry
because they did not follow him, and he suspected, moreover, that Lord Wenlock was intending to betray the queen and go over to the
other side; so he turned back in a rage, and,
coming up to Lord Wenlock, struck him a
dreadful blow upon his helmet with his battle-
axe, and killed him on the spot.

In the midst of the confusion which this affair produced, Richard, at the head of his brother's troops, came forcing his way into the in-
trenchments, bearing down all before him.
The queen's army was thrown into confusion,
and put to flight. Thousands upon thousands
were killed. As many as could save themselves from being slaughtered upon the spot
fled into the country toward the north, pursued
by detached parties of their enemies.

The young Prince of Wales was taken prisoner. The queen fled, and for a time it was
not known what had become of her. She fled
to the church in Tewkesbury, and took refuge
there.

As for the Prince of Wales, the account of

CHURCH AT TEWKESBURY.

his fate which was given at the time, and has generally been believed since, is this : As soon as the battle was over, he was brought, disarmed and helpless, into King Edward's tent, and there Edward, Clarence, Gloucester, and others gathered around to triumph over him, and taunt him with his downfall. Edward came up to him, and, after gazing upon him a moment in a fierce and defiant manner, demanded of him, in a furious tone, " What brought him to England?"

" My father's crown and my own inheritance," replied the prince.

Edward uttered some exclamation of anger, and then struck the prince upon the mouth with his gauntlet.*

At this signal, Gloucester, and the others who were standing by, fell upon the poor helpless boy, and killed him on the spot. The prince cried to Clarence, who was his brother-in-law, to save him, but in vain; Clarence did not interfere.

Some of the modern defenders of Richard's character attempt to show that there is no sufficient evidence that this story is true, and they

---

* The gauntlet was a sort of iron glove, the fingers of which were made flexible by joints formed with scales sliding over each other.

maintain that the prince was slain upon the
field, after the battle, and that Richard was innocent of his death. The evidence, however,
seems strongly against this last supposition.

Soon after the battle, it was found that the
queen, with her attendants, as has already been
stated, had taken refuge in a church at Tewkesbury, and in other sacred structures near.

Edward proceeded directly to the church,
with the intention of hunting out his enemies
wherever he could find them. He broke into
the sacred precincts, sword in hand, attended
by a number of reckless and desperate followers, and would have slain those that had taken
refuge there, on the spot, had not the abbot
himself come forward and interposed to protect
them. He came dressed in his sacerdotal robes,
and bearing the sacred emblems in his hands.
These emblems he held up before the infuriated
Edward as a token of the sanctity of the place.
By these means the king's hand was stayed,
and, before allowing him to go away, the abbot
exacted from him a promise that he would mo-
lest the refugees no more.

This promise was, however, not made to be
kept. Two days afterward Edward appointed
a court-martial, and sent Richard, with an armed
force, to the church, to take all the men that

QUEEN MARGARET BROUGHT IN PRISONER AT COVENTRY.

had sought refuge there, and bring them out for .
trial. The trial was conducted with very little
ceremony, and the men were all beheaded on
the green, in Tewkesbury, that very day.

Queen Margaret and the ladies who attended her were not with them. They had sought
refuge in another place. They were, however,
found after a few days, and were all brought
prisoners to Edward's camp at Coventry; for,
after the battle, Edward had begun to move on
with his army across the country.

The king's first idea was to send Margaret
immediately to London and put her in the Tower; but, before he did this, a change in his plans
took place, which led him to decide to go to
London himself. So he took Queen Margaret
with him, a captive in his train. On the arrival of the party in London, the queen was conveyed at once to the Tower.

Here she remained a close prisoner for five
long and weary years, and was then ransomed
by the King of France and taken to the Continent. She lived after this in comparative obscurity for about ten years, and then died.

As for her husband, his earthly troubles were
brought to an end much sooner. The cause of
the change of plan above referred to, which led
Edward to go directly to London soon after

9—11

the battle of Tewkesbury, was the news that a
relative of Warwick, whom that nobleman, during his life-time, had put in command in the
southeastern part of England, had raised an insurrection there, with a view of marching to
London, rescuing Henry from the Tower, and
putting him upon the throne. This movement
was soon put down, and Edward returned from
the expedition triumphant to London. He and
his brothers spent the night after their arrival
in the Tower. The next morning King Henry
was found dead in his bed.

The universal belief was then, and has been
since, that he was put to death by Edward's orders, and it has been the general opinion that
Richard was the murderer.

The body of the king was put upon a bier
that same day, and conveyed to St. Paul's
Church in London, and there exhibited to the
public for a long time, with guards and torch-
bearers surrounding it. An immense concourse
of people came to view his remains. The object of this exposition of the body of the king
was to make sure the fact of his death in the
public mind, and prevent the possibility of the
circulation of rumors, subsequently, by the partisans of his house, that he was still alive; for
such rumors would greatly have increased the

Burial of Henry VI.

danger of any insurrectionary plans which might be formed against Edward's authority.

In due time the body was interred at Windsor, and a sculptured monument, adorned with various arms and emblems, was erected over the tomb.

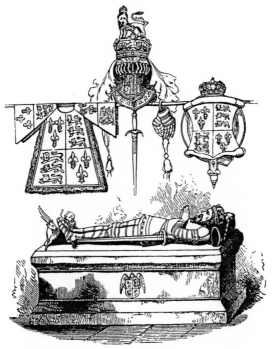

11   TOMB OF HENRY VI.

The remaining leaders on the Lancaster side were disposed of in a very effectual manner, to prevent the possibility of their again acquiring power. Some were banished. Others were shut up in various castles as hopeless prisoners. The country was thus wholly subdued, and Edward was once more established firmly on his throne.

CHAPTER VIII.

RICHARD'S MARRIAGE.

WHEN the affairs of the kingdom were settled, after the return of King Edward to the throne, Richard, Duke of Gloucester, the subject of the present volume, was found occupying a very exalted and brilliant position. It is true, he was yet very young, being only about nineteen years of age, and by birth he was second to Clarence, Clarence being his older brother. But Clarence had been so wavering and vacillating, having changed sides so often in the great quarrels, that no confidence was placed in him now on either side. Richard, on the other hand, had steadily adhered to his brother Edward's cause. He had shared all his brother's reverses, and he had rendered him most valuable and efficient aid in all the battles which he had fought, and had contributed essentially to his success in all the victories which he had gained. Of course, now, Edward and his friends had great confidence in Richard, while Clarence was looked upon with suspicion and distrust.

.Clarence, it is true, had one excuse for his instability, which Richard had not; for Clarence, having married the Earl of Warwick's daughter, was, of course, brought into very close connection with the earl, and was subjected greatly to his influence. Accordingly, whatever course Warwick decided to take, it was extremely difficult for Clarence to avoid joining him in it; and when at length Warwick arranged the marriage of his daughter Anne with the Prince of Wales, King Henry's son, and so joined himself to the Lancaster party, Clarence was placed between two strong and contrary attractions — his attachment to his brother, and his natural interest in the advancement of his own family being on one side, and his love for his wife, and the great influence and ascendency exerted over his mind by his father-in-law being on the other.

Richard was in no such strait There was nothing to entice him away from his fidelity to his brother, so he remained true.

He had been so brave and efficient, too, in the military operations connected with Edward's recovery of the throne, that he had acquired great renown as a soldier throughout the kingdom. The fame of his exploits was the more brilliant on account of his youth. It was con-

Richard made Lord High Admiral of England.

sidered remarkable that a young man not yet
out of his teens should show so much skill,
and act with so much resolution and energy in
times so trying, and the country resounded
with his praises.

As soon as Edward was established on the
throne, he raised Richard to what was in those
days, perhaps, the highest office under the
crown, that of Lord High Admiral of England.
This was the office which the Earl of Warwick
had held, and to which a great portion of the
power and influence which he exercised was
owing. The Lord High Admiral had command
of the navy, and of the principal ports on both
sides of the English Channel, so long as any
ports on the French side remained in English
hands. The reader will recollect, perhaps, that
while Richard was quite a small boy, his mother was compelled to fly with him and his little
brother George to France, to escape from the
enemies of the family, at the time of his father's
death, and that it was through the Earl of Warwick's co-operation that she was enabled to accomplish this flight. Now it was in consequence of Warwick's being at that time Lord
High Admiral of England, and his having command of Calais, and the waters between Calais
and England, that he could make arrangements

to assist Lady Cecily so effectually on that occasion.

Still, Richard, though universally applauded
for his military courage and energy, was known
to all who had opportunities of becoming personally acquainted with him to be a bad man.
He was unprincipled, hard-hearted, and reckless. This, however, did not detract from his
military fame. Indeed, depravity of private
character seldom diminishes much the applause
which a nation bestows upon those who acquire
military renown in their service. It is not to
be expected that it should. Military exploits
have been, in fact, generally, in the history of
the world, gigantic crimes, committed by reckless and remorseless men for the benefit of others, who, though they would be deterred by
their scruples of conscience or their moral sen-
sibilities from perpetrating such deeds themselves, are ready to repay, with the most ex-
travagant honors and rewards, those who are
ferocious and unscrupulous enough to perpe-
trate them in their stead. Were it not for some
very few and rare exceptions to the general
rule, which have from time to time appeared,
the history of mankind would show that, to be
a *good soldier*, it is almost absolutely essential to
be a *bad man*.

The child, Prince Edward, the son of Edward the Fourth, who was born, as is related in a preceding chapter, in the sanctuary at Westminster, whither his mother had fled at the time when Edward was expelled from the kingdom, was, of course, King Edward's heir. He was now less than a year old, and, in order to place his title to the crown beyond dispute, a solemn oath was required from all the leading nobles and officers of Edward's government, that in case he survived his father they would acknowledge him as king. The following is the form of the oath which was taken :

I acknowledge, take, and repute you, Edward, Prince of Wales, Duke of Cornwayll, and Erl of Chestre, furste begoten son of oure sovereigne lord, as to the corones and reames of England and of France, and lordship of Ireland; and promette and swere that in case hereafter it happen you by Goddis disposition do outlive our sovereigne lord, I shall then take and accept you for true, veray and righteous King of England, and of France, and of Ireland; and feith and trouth to you shall bere, and yn all thyngs truely and feithfully behave me towardes you and youre heyres, as a true and feithful subject oweth to behave him to his sovereigne lord and rightfllys King of England, France, and Ireland; so help me God, and Holdome, and this holy Evangelist.

Richard took this oath with the rest. How he kept it will hereafter appear.

The Lady Anne, the second daughter of the
Earl of Warwick, who had been betrothed to
the Prince of Wales, King Henry's son, was
left, by the fall of the house of Lancaster and
the re-establishment of King Edward the Fourth
upon the throne, in a most forlorn and pitiable
condition. Her father, the earl, was dead, having been killed in battle. Her betrothed husband, too, the Prince of Wales, with whom she
had fondly hoped one day to sit on the throne
of England, had been cruelly assassinated.
Queen Margaret, the mother of the prince, who
might have been expected to take an interest
in her fate, was a helpless prisoner in the Tower. And if the fallen queen had been at liberty, it is very probable that all her interest in
Anne would prove to have been extinguished
by the death of her son; for Queen Margaret
had never felt any personal preference for Anne,
and had only consented to the marriage very
reluctantly, and from political considerations
alone. The friends and connections of her father's family, a short time since so exalted in
station and so powerful, were now scattered
and destroyed. Some had been killed in battle, others beheaded by executioners, others
banished from the realm. The rest were roam-
ing about England in terror and distress, house-

less, homeless, friendless, and only intent to find some hiding-place where they might screen themselves from Edward's power and vengeance.

There was one exception, indeed, the Lady Isabella, Clarence's wife, who, as the reader will recollect, was Warwick's oldest daughter, and, of course, the sister of Lady Anne. She and Clarence, her husband, it might be supposed, would take an interest in Lady Anne's fate. Indeed, Clarence did take an interest in it, but, unfortunately, the interest was of the wrong kind.

The Earl of Warwick had been immensely wealthy. Besides the ancient stronghold of the family, Warwick Castle, one of the most renowned old feudal fortresses in England, he owned many other castles, and many large estates, and rights of property of various kinds all over the kingdom. Now Clarence, after Warwick's death, had taken most of this property into his own hands as the husband of the earl's oldest daughter, and he wished to keep it. This he could easily do while Anne remained in her present friendless and helpless condition. But he knew very well that if she were to be married to any person of rank and influence on the York side, her husband would

insist on a division of the property. Now he
suspected that his brother Richard had conceived the design of marrying her. He accordingly set himself at work earnestly to thwart
this design.

It was true that Richard had conceived the
idea of making Anne his wife, from the motive, however, solely, as it would seem, to obtain her share of her father's property.

Richard had been acquainted with Anne from
her childhood. Indeed, he was related to the
family of the Earl of Warwick on his mother's
side. His mother, Lady Cecily Neville, belonged to the same great family of Neville from
which the Warwicks sprung. Warwick had
been a great friend of Lady Cecily in former
years, and it is even supposed that when Richard and his brother George were brought back
from the Continent, at the time when Edward
first obtained possession of the kingdom, they
lived for a time in Warwick's family at Middleham Castle.* This is not quite certainly
known, but it is at any rate known that Richard and Anne knew each other well when they
were children, and were often together.

There is an account of a grand entertainment

* For a view of this castle, and the grounds pertaining to
it, see page 180.

which was given by the Warwick family at
York, some years before, on the occasion of
the enthroning of the earl's brother George as
Archbishop of York, at which Richard was
present. Richard, being a prince of the blood
royal, was, of course, a very highly honored
guest, notwithstanding that he was but a child.
So they prepared for him and some few other great personages a raised platform, called a
dais, at one end of the banquet-hall, with a royal canopy over it. The table for the distinguished personages was upon this dais, while
those for the other guests extended up and
down the hall below. Richard was seated at
the centre of the table of honor, with a countess
on one side of him and a duchess on the other.
Opposite to him, at the same table, were seated
Isabella and Anne. Anne was at this time
about twelve years old.

Now it is supposed that Isabella and Anne
were placed at this table to please Richard, for
their mother, who was, of course, entitled to
take precedence of them, had her seat at one of
the large tables below.

From this and some other similar indications, it is supposed that Richard took a fancy
to Anne while they were quite young, as Clarence did to Isabella. Indeed, one of the ancient

writers says that Richard wished, at this early period, to choose her for his wife, but that she did not like him.

At any rate, now, after the re-establishment of his brother upon the throne, and his own exaltation to such high office under him, he determined that he would marry Anne. Clarence, on the other hand, determined that he should not marry her. So Clarence, with the pretense of taking her under his protection, seized her, and carried her away to a place of concealment, where he kept her closely shut up. Anne consented to this, for she wished to keep out of Richard's way. Richard's person was disagreeable to her, and his character was hateful. She seems to have considered him, as he is generally represented by the writers of those times, as a rude, hard-hearted, and unscrupulous man; and she had also a special reason for shrinking from him with horror, as the mortal enemy of her father, and the reputed murderer of the husband to whom she had been betrothed.

Clarence kept her for some time in obscure places of concealment, changing the place from time to time to elude the vigilance of Richard, who was continually making search for her. The poor princess had recourse to all manner

of contrivances, and assumed the most humble
disguises to keep herself concealed, and was at
last reduced to a very forlorn and destitute condition, through the desperate shifts that she re-
sorted to, in her endeavors to escape Richard's
persecutions. All was, however, in vain. Richard discovered her at last in a mean house in
London, where she was living in the disguise
of a servant. He immediately seized her, and
conveyed her to a place of security which was
under his control.

Soon after this she was taken away from this
place and conveyed to York, and placed, for
the time, under the protection of the archbishop
—the same archbishop at whose enthronement,
eight or ten years before, she had sat at the
same table with Richard, under the royal canopy. But she was not left at peace here. Richard insisted on her marrying him. She insisted on her refusal. Her friends—the few that
she had left—turned against her, and urged her
to consent to the union; but she could not endure the thought of it.

Richard, however, persisted in his determination, and Anne was finally overcome. It is said
she resisted to the last, and that the ceremony
was performed by compulsion, Anne continuing
to refuse her consent to the end. It was fore-

RICHARD III.

seen that, as soon as any change of circumstances should enable her to resume active resistance to the union, she would repudiate the
marriage altogether, as void for want of her
consent, or else obtain a divorce. To guard
against this danger, Richard procured the passage of an act of Parliament, by which he was
empowered to continue in the full possession
and enjoyment of Anne's property, even if *she*

Difficulty about the division of the property.

QUEEN ANNE.

were to divorce him, provided that he did his best
to be reconciled to her, and was willing to be
re-married to her, with her consent, whenever
she was willing to grant it.

As for Richard himself, his object was fully
attained by the accomplishment of a marriage
so far acknowledged as to entitle him to the
possession of the property of his wife.   There
was still some difficulty, however, arising from
a disagreement between Richard and Clarence
in respect to the division.   Clarence, when he

9—12

found that Richard would marry Anne, in spite
of all that he could do to prevent it, declared,
with an oath, that, even if Richard did marry
her, he, Clarence, would never " part the liveli-
hood," that is, divide the property with him.

So fixed was Clarence in this resolution to
retain all the property himself, and so resolute
was Richard, on the other hand, in his determination to have his share, that the quarrel very
soon assumed a very serious character. The
lords and nobles of the court took part in the
controversy on one side and on the other, until, at length, there was imminent danger of
open war. Finally Edward himself interposed,
and summoned the brothers to appear before
him in open council, when, after a full hearing
of the dispute, he said that he himself would
decide the question. Accordingly, the two
brothers appeared before the king, and each
strenuously argued his own cause. The king,
after hearing them, decided how the property
should be divided. He gave to Richard and
Anne a large share, but not all that Richard
claimed. Richard was, however, compelled to
submit.

When the marriage was thus consummated,
and Richard had been put in possession of his
portion of the property, Anne seems to have

MIDDLEHAM CASTLE.

submitted to her fate, and she went with Richard to Middleham Castle, in the north of England. This castle was one which had belonged to the Warwick family, and it now came
into Richard's possession. Richard did not,
however, remain long here with his wife. He
went away on various military expeditions,
leaving Anne most of the time alone. She
was well contented to be thus left, for nothing
could be so welcome to her now as to be relieved as much as possible from the presence of
her hateful husband.

This state of things continued, without much
change, until the end of about a year after her
marriage, when Anne gave birth to a son. The
boy was named Edward. The possession of
this treasure awakened in the breast of Anne
a new interest in life, and repaid her, in some
measure, for the sorrows and sufferings which
she had so long endured.

. Her love for her babe, in fact, awakened in
her heart something like a tie to bind her to
her husband. It is hard for a mother to continue long to hate the father of her child.

CHAPTER IX.

END OF THE REIGN OF EDWARD.

KING EDWARD reigned, after this time, for about eight years. During this period, Richard continued to occupy a very high official position, and a very conspicuous place in the public mind. He was generally considered as personally a very bad man, and, whenever any great public crime was committed, in which the government were implicated at all, it was Richard, usually, who was supposed to be chiefly instrumental in the perpetration of it; but, notwithstanding this, his fame, and the general consideration in which he was held, were very high. This was owing, in a considerable degree, to his military renown, and the straightforward energy and decision which characterized all his doings.

He generally co-operated very faithfully in all Edward's plans and schemes, though sometimes, when he thought them calculated to impede rather than promote the interests of the kingdom and the aggrandizement of the family, he made no secret of opposing them. As to

Clarence, no one placed any trust or confidence in him whatever. For a time, he and Edward were ostensibly on friendly terms with each other, but there was no cordial good-will between them. Each watched the other with continual suspicion and distrust.

About the year 1475, Edward formed a grand scheme for the invasion of France, in order to recover from the French king certain possessions which Edward claimed, on the ground of their having formerly belonged to his ancestors. This plan, as, indeed, almost all plans of war and conquest were in those days, was very popular in England, and arrangements were made on an immense scale for fitting out an expedition. The Duke of Burgundy, who, as will be recollected, had married Edward's sister, promised to join the English in this proposed war. When all was ready, the English army set sail, and crossed over to Calais. Edward went with the army as commander-in-chief. He was accompanied by Clarence and Gloucester. Thus far every thing had gone on well, and all Europe was watching with great interest for the result of the expedition; but, very soon after landing, great difficulties arose. The Duke of Burgundy and Edward disagreed, and this disagreement caused great

delays.   The army advanced slowly toward
the French frontier, but for two months nothing effectual was done.

In the mean time, Louis, the King of France,

LOUIS XI. OF FRANCE.

who was a very shrewd and wily man, concluded that it would be better for him to buy off
his enemies than to fight them.   So he continually sent messengers and negotiators to Edward's camp with proposals of various sorts,
made to gain time, in order to enable him, by

means of presents and bribes, to buy up all the
prominent leaders and counselors of the expedition.   He gave secretly to all the men who
he supposed held an influence over Edward's
mind, large sums of money.   He offered, too, to
make a treaty with Edward, by which, under
one pretext or another, he was to pay him a
great deal of money.   One of these proposed
payments was that of a large sum for the ransom of Queen Margaret, as mentioned in a preceding chapter.   The amount of the ransom
money which he proposed was fifty thousand
crowns.

Besides these promises to pay money in case
the treaty was concluded, Louis made many
rich and valuable presents at once.   One day,
while the negotiations were pending, he sent
over to the English camp, as a gift to the king,
three hundred cart-loads of wine, the best that
could be procured in the kingdom.

At one time, near the beginning of the affair,
when a herald was sent to Louis from Edward
with a very defiant and insolent message, Louis, instead of resenting the message as an affront,
entertained the herald with great politeness,
held a long and friendly conversation with him,
and finally sent him away with three hundred
crowns in his purse, and a promise of a thou-

sand more as soon as a peace should be concluded. He also made him a present of a piece
of crimson velvet "thirty ells long." Such a
gift as this of the crimson velvet was calculated,
perhaps, in those days of military foppery, to
please the herald even more than the money.

These things, of course, put Edward and
nearly all his followers in excellent humor, and
disposed them to listen very favorably to any
propositions for settling the quarrel which Louis might be disposed to make. At last, after
various and long protracted negotiations, a
treaty was agreed upon, and Louis proposed
that at the final execution of it he and Edward
should have a personal interview.

Edward acceded to this on certain conditions,
and the circumstances under which the interview took place, and the arrangements which
were adopted on the occasion, make it one of
the most curious transactions of the whole reign.

It seems that Edward could not place the
least trust in Louis's professions of friendship,
and did not dare to meet him without requiring beforehand most extraordinary precautions
to guard against the possibility of treachery.
So it was agreed that the meeting should take
place upon a bridge, Louis and his friends to
come in upon one side of the bridge, and Ed-

The grating on the bridge.

ward, with his party, on the other. In order
to prevent either party from seizing and carrying off the other, there was a strong barricade
of wood built across the bridge in the middle
of it, and the arrangement was for the King of
France to come up to this barricade on one side,
and the King of England on the other, and so
shake hands and communicate with each other
through the bars of the barricade.

The place where this most extraordinary royal meeting was held was called Picquigny, and
the treaty which was made there is known in
history as the Treaty of Picquigny. The town
is on the River Somme, near the city of Amiens. Amiens was at that time very near the
French frontier.

The day appointed for the meeting was the
29th of August, 1475. The barricade was prepared. It was made of strong bars, crossing
each other so as to form a grating, such as was
used in those days to make the cages of bears,
and lions, and other wild beasts. The spaces
between the bars were only large enough to allow a man's arm to pass through.

The King of France went first to the grating,
advancing, of course, from the French side. He
was accompanied by ten or twelve attendants,
all men of high rank and station. He was very

splendidly dressed for the occasion. The dress was made of cloth of gold, with a large *fleur de lis*—which was at that time the emblem of the French sovereignty — magnificently worked upon it in precious stones.

When Louis and his party had reached the barricade, Edward, attended likewise by his friends, approached on the other side. When they came to the barricade, the two kings greeted each other with many bows and other salutations, and they also shook hands with each other by reaching through the grating. The King of France addressed Edward in a very polite and courteous manner. " Cousin," said he, " you are right welcome. There is no person living that I have been so ambitious of seeing as you, and God be thanked that our interview now is on so happy an occasion."

After these preliminary salutations and cere-monies had been concluded, a prayer-book, or missal, as it was called, and a crucifix, were brought forward, and held at the grating where both kings could touch them. Each of the kings then put his hands upon them—one hand on the crucifix and the other on the missal—and they both took a solemn oath by these sacred emblems that they would faithfully keep the treaty which they had made.

After thus transacting the business which had
brought them together, the two kings conversed
with each other in a gay and merry manner for
some time. The King of France invited Edward to come to Paris and make him a visit.
This, of course, was a joke, for Edward would
as soon think of accepting an invitation from a
lion to come and visit him in his den, as of putting himself in Louis's power by going to Paris.
Both monarchs and all the attendants laughed
merrily at this jest. Louis assured Edward
that he would have a very pleasant time at
Paris in amusing himself with the gay ladies,
and in other dissipations. "And then here is
the cardinal," he added, turning to the Cardinal
of Bourbon, an ecclesiastic of very high rank,
but of very loose character, who was among his
attendants, "who will grant you a very easy
absolution for any sins you may take a fancy
to commit while you are there."

Edward and his friends were much amused
with this sportive conversation of Louis's, and
Edward made many smart replies, especially
joking the cardinal, who, he knew, "was a gay
man with the ladies, and a boon companion over
his wine."

This sort of conversation continued for some
time, and at length the kings, after again shak-

ing hands through the grating, departed each his own way, and thus this most extraordinary conference of sovereigns was terminated.

The treaty which was thus made at the bridge of Picquigny contained several very important articles. The principal of them were the following:

1. Louis was to pay fifty thousand crowns as a ransom for Queen Margaret, and Edward was to release her from the Tower and send her to France as soon as he arrived in England.

2. Louis was to pay to Edward in cash, on the spot, seventy-five thousand crowns, and an annuity of fifty thousand crowns.

3. He was to marry his son, the dauphin, to Edward's oldest daughter, Elizabeth, and, in case of her death, then to his next daughter, Mary. These parties were all children at this time, and so the actual marriage was postponed for a time; but it was stipulated solemnly that it should be performed as soon as the prince and princess attained to a proper age. It is important to remember this part of the treaty, as a great and serious difficulty grew out of it when the time for the execution of it arrived.

4. By the last article, the two kings bound themselves to a truce for seven years, during which time hostilities were to be entirely sus-

pended, and free trade between the two countries was to be allowed.

Clarence was with the king at the time of
making this treaty, and he joined with the other courtiers in giving it his approval, but Richard would have nothing to do with it. He very
much preferred to go on with the war, and was
indignant that his brother should allow himself
to be bought off, as it were, by presents and
payments of money, and induced to consent to
what seemed to him an ignominious peace. He
did not give any open expression to his discon-
tent, but he refused to be present at the conference on the bridge, and, when Edward and the
army, after the peace was concluded, went back
to England, he went with them, but in very bad
humor.

The people of England were in very bad
humor too. You will observe that the induce-
ments which Louis employed in procuring the
treaty were gifts and sums of money granted
to Edward himself, and to his great courtiers
personally for their own private uses. There
was nothing in his concessions which tended
at all to the aggrandizement or to the benefit
of the English realm, or to promote the interest
of the people at large. They thought, therefore, that Edward and his counselors had been

induced to sacrifice the rights and honor of the
crown and the kingdom to their own personal
advantage by a system of gross and open brib-
ery, and they were very much displeased.

The next great event which marks the history of the reign of Edward, after the conclusion of this war, was the breaking out anew of
the old feud between Edward and Clarence, and
the dreadful crisis to which the quarrel finally
reached. The renewal of the quarrel began in
Edward's dispossessing Clarence of a portion of
his property. Edward was very much embar-
rassed for money after his return from the
French expedition. He had incurred great
debts in fitting out the expedition, and these
debts the Parliament and people of England
were very unwilling to pay, on account of their
being so much displeased with the peace which
had been made. Edward, consequently, notwithstanding the bribes which he had received
from Louis, was very much in want of money.
At last he caused a law to be passed by Parliament enacting that all the patrimony of the
royal family, which had hitherto been divided
among the three brothers, should be resumed,
and applied to the service of the crown. This
made Clarence very angry. True, he was ex-

tremely rich, through the property which he
had received by his wife from the Warwick
estates, but this did not make him any more
willing to submit patiently to be robbed by his
brother. He expressed his anger very openly,
and the ill feeling which the affair occasioned
led to a great many scenes of dispute and crim-
ination between the two brothers, until at last
Clarence could no longer endure to have any
thing to do with Edward, and he went away,
with Isabella his wife, to a castle which he possessed near Tewkesbury, and there remained,
in angry and sullen seclusion. So great was
the animosity that prevailed at this time between the brothers and their respective partisans, that almost every one who took an active
part in the quarrel lived in continual anxiety
from fear of being poisoned, or of being destroyed by incantations or witchcraft.

Every body believed in witchcraft in these
days. There was one peculiar species of necromancy which was held in great dread. It
was supposed that certain persons had the power secretly to destroy any one against whom
they conceived a feeling of ill will in the following manner: They would first make an effigy of their intended victim out of wax and
other similar materials. This image was made

9—13

the representation of the person to be destroyed by means of certain sorceries and incantations, and then it was by slow degrees, from day
to day, melted away and gradually destroyed.
While the image was thus melting, the innocent and unconscious victim of the witchcraft
would pine away, and at last, when the image
was fairly gone, would die.

Not very long after Clarence left the court
and went to Tewkesbury, his wife gave birth to
a child. It was the second son. The child was
named Richard, and is known in history as
Richard of Clarence. Isabella did not recover
her health and strength after the birth of her
child. She pined away in a slow and lingering manner for two or three months, and then
died.

Clarence was convinced that she did not die
a natural death. He believed that her life had
been destroyed by some process of witchcraft,
such as has been described, or by poison, and
he openly charged the queen with having in-
stigated the murder by having employed some
sorcerer or assassin to accomplish it. After a
time he satisfied himself that a certain woman
named Ankaret Twynhyo was the person
whom the queen had employed to commit this
crime, and watching an opportunity when this

woman was at her own residence, away from all who could protect her, he sent a body of armed men from among his retainers, who went secretly to the place, and, breaking in suddenly, seized the woman and bore her off to Warwick Castle. There Clarence subjected her to what he called a trial, and she was condemned to death, and executed at once. The charge against her was that she administered poison to the duchess in a cup of ale. So summary were these proceedings, that the poor woman was dead in three hours from the time that she arrived at the castle gates.

These proceedings, of course, greatly exasperated Edward and the queen, and made them hate Clarence more than ever.

Very soon after this, Charles, the Duke of Burgundy, who married Margaret, Edward and Clarence's sister, and who had been Edward's ally in so many of his wars, was killed in battle. He left a daughter named Mary, of whom Margaret was the step-mother; for Mary was the child of the duke by a former marriage. Now, as Charles was possessed of immense estates, Mary, by his death, became a great heiress, and Clarence, now that his wife was dead, conceived the idea of making her his second wife. He immediately commenced negotia-

13

tions to this end. Margaret favored the plan, but Edward and Elizabeth, the queen, as soon as they heard of it, set themselves at work in the most earnest manner to thwart and circumvent it.

Their motives for opposing this match arose partly from their enmity to Clarence, and partly from designs of their own which they had formed in respect to the marriage of Mary. The queen wished to secure the young heiress for one of her brothers. Edward had another plan, which was to marry Mary to a certain Duke Maximilian. Edward's plan, in the end, was carried out, and Clarence was defeated. When Clarence found at length that the bride, with all the immense wealth and vastly increased importance which his marriage with her was to bring, were lost to him through Edward's interference, and conferred upon his hated rival Maximilian, he was terribly enraged. He expressed his resentment and anger against the king in the most violent terms.

About this time a certain nobleman, one of the king's friends, died. The king accused a priest, who was in Clarence's service, of having killed him by sorcery. The priest was seized and put to the torture to compel him to confess his crime and to reveal his confederates. The priest at length confessed, and named as his accomplice one of Clarence's household named Burdett, a gentleman who lived in very intimate and confidential relations with Clarence himself.

The confession was taken as proof of guilt, and the priest and Burdett were both immediately executed.

Clarence was now perfectly frantic with rage. He could restrain himself no longer. He forced his way into the king's council-chamber, and there uttered to the lords who were assembled the most violent and angry denunciation of the king. He accused him of injustice and cruelty, and upbraided him, and all who counseled and aided him, in the severest terms.

When the king, who was not himself present on this occasion, heard what Clarence had done, he said that such proceedings were subversive of the laws of the realm, and destructive to all good government, and he commanded that Clarence should be arrested and sent to the Tower.

After a short time the king summoned a Parliament, and when the assembly was convened, he brought his brother out from his prison in the Tower, and arraigned him at the bar of the House of Lords on charges of the most extraordinary character, which he himself personally

preferred against him. In these charges Clarence was accused of having formed treasonable
conspiracies to depose the king, disinherit the
king's children, and raise himself to the throne,
and with this view of having slandered the
king, and endeavored, by bribes and false representations, to entice away his subjects from
their allegiance; of having joined himself with
the Lancastrian faction so far as to promise to
restore them their estates which had been confiscated, provided that they would assist him in
usurping the throne; and of having secretly organized an armed force, which was all ready,
and waiting only for the proper occasion to
strike the blow.

Clarence denied all these charges in the most
earnest and solemn manner. The king insisted
upon the truth of them, and brought forward
many witnesses to prove them. Of course,
whether the charges were true or false, there
could be no difficulty in finding plenty of witnesses to give the required testimony. The
lords listened to the charges and the defense
with a sort of solemn awe. Indeed, all England,
as it were, stood by, silenced and appalled at the
progress of this dreadful fraternal quarrel, and
at the prospect of the terrible termination of it,
which all could foresee must come.

THE MURDERERS COMING FOR CLARENCE.

He is sentenced to death.   He is assassinated.

Whatever the members of Parliament may have thought of the truth or falsehood of the charges, there was only one way in which it was prudent or even safe for them to vote, and Clarence was condemned to death.

Sentence being passed, the prisoner was remanded to the Tower.

Edward seems, after all, to have shrunk from the open and public execution of the sentence which he had caused to be pronounced against his brother. No public execution took place, but in a short time it was announced that Clarence had died in prison. It was understood that assassins were employed to go privately into the room where he was confined and put him to death; and it is universally believed, though there is no positive proof of the fact, that Richard was the person who made the arrangements for the performance of this deed.*

After Clarence was dead, and the excitement and anger of the quarrel had subsided in Edward's mind, he was overwhelmed with remorse and anguish at what he had done. He attempt-

* There was a strange story in respect to the manner of Clarence's death, which was very current at the time, namely, that he was drowned by his brothers in a butt of Malmsey wine. But there is no evidence whatever that this story was true.

ed to drown these painful thoughts by dissipa-
tion and vice. He neglected the affairs of his
government, and his duties to his wife and family, and spent his time in gay pleasures with
the ladies of his court, and in guilty carousings
with wicked men. In these pleasures he spent
large sums of money, wasting his patrimony
and all his resources in extravagance and folly.
Among other amusements, he used to form
hunting-parties, in which the ladies of his court
were accustomed to join, and he used to set up
gay silken tents for their accommodation on
the hunting-ground. He spent vast sums, too,
upon his dress, being very vain of his personal
attractions, and of the favor in which he was
held by the ladies around him.

The most conspicuous of his various female
favorites was the celebrated Jane Shore. She
was the wife of a respectable citizen of London.
Edward enticed her away from her husband,
and induced her to come and live at court with
him. The opposite engraving, which is taken
from an ancient portrait, gives undoubtedly a
correct representation both of her features and
of her dress. We shall hear more of this person in the sequel.

Things went on in this way for about two
years, when at length war broke out on the

Edward sends Richard to war.

JANE SHORE.

frontiers of Scotland.   Edward was too much
engrossed with his gallantries and pleasures to
march himself to meet the enemy, and so he
commissioned Richard to go.   Richard was
very well pleased that his brother Edward
should remain at home, and waste away in ef-
feminacy and vice his character and his influ-

ence in the kingdom, while he went forth in command of the army, to acquire, by the vigor and success of his military career, that ascendency that Edward was losing. So he took the command of the army and went forth to the war.

The war was protracted for several years. The King of Scotland had a brother, the Duke of Albany, who was attempting to dethrone him, in order that he might reign in his stead; that is, he was doing exactly that which Edward had charged upon his brother Clarence, and for which he had caused Clarence to be killed ; and yet, with strange inconsistency, Edward espoused the cause of this Clarence of Scotland, and laid deep plans for enabling him to depose and supplant his brother.

In the midst of the measures which Richard was taking for the execution of these plans, they, as well as all Edward's other earthly schemes and hopes, were suddenly destroyed by the hand of death. Edward's health had become much impaired by the dissolute life which he had led, and at last he fell seriously sick. While he was sick, an affair occurred which vexed and worried his mind beyond endurance.

The reader will recollect that, at the treaty which Edward made with Louis of France at the barricade on the bridge of Picquigny,

His anger against the King of France.

a marriage contract was concluded between
Louis's oldest son, the Dauphin of France, and
Edward's daughter Mary, and it was agreed
that, as soon as the children were grown up,
and were old enough, they should be married.
Louis took a solemn oath upon the prayer-book
and crucifix that he would not fail to keep this
agreement.

But now some years had passed away, and
circumstances had changed so much that Louis
did not wish to keep this promise.   Edward's
great ally, the Duke of Burgundy, was dead.
His daughter Mary, who became the Duchess
Mary on the death of her father, and who, so
greatly to Clarence's disappointment, had married Maximilian, had succeeded to the estates
and possessions of her father.   These possessions the King of France desired very much to
join to his dominions, as they lay contiguous
to them, and the fear of Edward, which had
prompted him to make the marriage contract
with him in the first instance, had now passed
away, on account of Edward's having become
so much weakened by his vices and his effemi-
nacy.   He now, therefore, became desirous of
allying his family to that of Burgundy rather
than that of England.

The Duchess Mary had three children, all

very young. The oldest, Philip, was only about three years old.

Now it happened that just at this time, while the Duchess Mary was out with a small party, hawking, near the city of Bruges, as they were flying the hawks at some herons, the company galloping on over the fields in order to keep up with the birds, the duchess's horse, in taking a leap, burst the girths of the saddle, and the duchess was thrown off against the trunk of a tree. She was immediately taken up and borne into a house, but she was so much injured that she almost immediately died.

Of course, her titles and estates would now descend to her children. The second of the children was a girl. Her name was Margaret. She was about two years old. Louis immediately resolved to give up the match between the dauphin and Edward's daughter Mary, and contract another alliance for him with this little Margaret. He met with considerable difficulty and delay in bringing this about, but he succeeded at last. While the negotiations were pending, Edward, who suspected what was going on, was assured that nothing of the kind was intended, and various false tales and pretenses were advanced by Louis to quiet his mind.

At length, when all was settled, the new plan was openly proclaimed, and great celebrations and parades were held in Paris in honor of the event. Edward was overwhelmed with vexation and rage when he received the tidings. He was, however, completely helpless. He lay tossing restlessly on his sick-bed, cursing, on the one hand, Louis's faithlessness and treachery, and, on the other, his own miserable weakness and pain, which made it so utterly impossible that he should do any thing to resent the affront.

His vexation and rage so disturbed and worried him that they hastened his death. When he found that his last hour was drawing near, a new source of agitation and anguish was opened in his mind by the remorse which now began to overwhelm him for his vices and crimes. Long-forgotten deeds of injustice, of violence, and of every species of wickedness rose before his mind, and terrified him with awful premonition of the anger of God and of the judgment to come. In his distress, he tried to make reparation for some of the grossest of the wrongs which he had committed, but it was too late. After lingering a week or two in this condition of distress and suffering, his spirit passed away.

CHAPTER X.

RICHARD AND EDWARD V.

AS the tidings of Edward's death spread throughout England, they were received every where with a sentiment of anxiety and suspense, for no one knew what the consequences would be. Edward left two sons. Edward, the oldest of the two, the Prince of Wales, was about thirteen years of age. The youngest, whose name was Richard, was eleven. Of course, Edward was the rightful heir to the crown. Next to him in the line of succession came his brother, and next to them came Richard, Duke of Gloucester, their uncle. But it was universally known that the Duke of Gloucester was a reckless and unscrupulous man, and the question in every one's mind was whether he would recognize the rights of his young nephews at all, or whether he would seize the crown at once for himself.

Richard, Duke of Gloucester, was in the northern part of England at this time, at the head of his army. The great power which the possession of this army gave him made people all the more fearful that he might attempt to usurp the throne.

The person who was most anxious in respect to the result was the widowed Queen Elizabeth, the mother of the two princes. She was very much alarmed. The boys themselves were not old enough to realize very fully the danger that they were in, or to render their mother much aid in her attempts to save them. The person on whom she chiefly relied was her brother, the Earl of Rivers. Edward, her oldest son, was under this uncle Rivers's care. The uncle and the nephew were residing together at this time at the castle of Ludlow.* Queen Elizabeth was in London with her second son.

Immediately on the death of the king, a council was called to deliberate upon the measures proper to be taken. The council decreed that the Prince of Wales should be proclaimed king, and they fixed upon the 4th of May for the day of his coronation. They also made arrangements for sending orders to the Earl of Rivers to come at once with the young king to London, in order that the coronation might take place.

Queen Elizabeth was present at this council, and she desired that her brother might be ordered to come attended by as large an armed

* For a view of this castle, see page 26.

9—14

force as he could raise, for the protection of the prince on the way.

Now it happened that there were great dissensions among the officers and nobles of the court at this time. The queen, with the relatives and connections of her family, formed one party, and the other nobles and peers of England another party, and great was the animosity and hatred that prevailed. The English nobles had never been satisfied with Edward's marriage, and they were very jealous of the influence of the queen's family and relations. This feud had been kept down in some degree while Edward lived, and Edward had made a great final effort to heal it entirely in his last sickness. He called together the leading nobles on each side, that had taken part in this quarrel, and then, by great exertion, went in among them, and urged them to forget their dissensions and become reconciled to each other. The effort for the time seemed to be successful, and both parties agreed to a compromise of the quarrel, and took a solemn oath that they would thenceforth live together in peace. But now, on the death of the king, the dissension broke out afresh. The other nobles were very jealous and suspicious of every measure which Elizabeth proposed, especially if it tended to

THE ATTEMPTED RECONCILIATION.

continue the possession of power and influence in the hands of her family. Accordingly, when she proposed in the council to send for the earl, and to require him to raise a large escort to bring the young Prince Edward to London, they objected to it.

"Against whom," demanded one of the councilors, "is the young prince to be defended? Who are his enemies? He has none, and the real motive and design of raising this force is not to protect the prince, but only to secure to the Woodville family the means of increasing and perpetuating their own importance and power."

The speaker upbraided the queen, too, with having, by this proposal, and by the attempt to promote the aggrandizement of the Woodville party which was concealed in it, been guilty of violating the oath of reconciliation which had been taken during the last sickness of the late king. So the council refused to authorize the armed escort, and the queen, with tears of disappointment and vexation, gave up the plan. At least she gave it up ostensibly, but she nevertheless contrived to come to some secret understanding with the earl, in consequence of which he set out from the castle with the young prince at the head of quite a large force. Some

of the authorities state that he had with him
two thousand men.

In the mean time, Richard of Gloucester, as
soon as he heard of Edward's death, arranged
his affairs at once, and made preparations to
set out for London too. He put his army in
mourning for the death of the king, and he
wrote a most respectful and feeling letter of
condolence to the queen. In this letter he
made a solemn profession of homage and fealty
to her son, the Prince of Wales, whom he acknowledged as rightfully entitled to the crown,
and promised to be faithful in his allegiance to
him, and to all the duties which he owed him.

Queen Elizabeth's mind was much relieved
by this letter. She began to think that she
was going to find in Richard an efficient friend
to sustain her cause and that of her family
against her enemies.

When Richard reached York, he made a solemn entry into that town, attended by six hundred knights all dressed in deep mourning. At
the head of this funeral procession he proceeded to the Cathedral, and there caused the obse-
quies of the king to be celebrated with great
pomp, and with very impressive and apparently
sincere exhibitions of the grief which he himself personally felt for the loss of his brother.

After a brief delay in York, Richard resumed his march to the southward. He arranged it so as to overtake the party of the prince and the Earl of Rivers on the way.

He arrived at the town of Northampton on the same day that the prince, with the Earl of Rivers and his escort, reached the town of Stony Stratford, which was only a few miles from it. When the earl heard that Gloucester was so near, he took with him another nobleman, named Lord Gray, and a small body of attendants, and rode back to Northampton to pay his respects to Gloucester on the part of the young king; for they considered that Edward became at once, by the death of his father, King of England, under the style and title of Edward the Fifth.

Gloucester received his visitors in a very courteous and friendly manner. He invited them to sup with him, and he made quite an entertainment for them, and for some other friends whom he invited to join them. The party spent the evening together in a very agreeable manner.

They sat so long over their wine that it was too late for the earl and Lord Gray to return that night to Stony Stratford, and Richard accordingly made arrangements for them to re-

main in Northampton. He assigned quarters
to them in the town, and secretly set a guard
over them, to prevent their making their escape.
The next morning, when they arose, they were
astonished to find themselves under guard, and
to perceive too, as they did, that all the avenues
of the town were occupied with troops. They
suspected treachery, but they thought it not
prudent to express their suspicions. Richard,
when he met them again in the morning, treated them in the same friendly manner as on the
evening before, and proposed to accompany
them to Stony Stratford, in order that he might
there see and pay his respects to the king.
This was agreed to, and they all set out together.

In company with Richard was one of his
friends and confederates, the Duke of Buckingham. This Duke of Buckingham had been
one of the leaders of the party at court that
were opposed to the family of the queen. These
two, together with the Earl of Rivers and Lord
Gray, rode on in a very friendly manner toward Stratford. They went in advance of Richard's troops, which were ordered to follow pretty closely behind. In this manner they went
on till they began to draw near to the town.

Richard now at once threw off his disguise.

He told the Earl of Rivers and Lord Gray that
the influence which they were exerting over
the mind of the king was evil, and that he felt
it his duty to take the king from their charge.

Then, at a signal given, armed men came up
and took the two noblemen in custody. Richard, with the Duke of Buckingham and their
attendants, drove on with all speed into the
town. It seems that the persons who had been
left with Edward had, in some way or other,
obtained intelligence of what was going on, for
they were just upon the eve of making their
escape with him when Richard and his party
arrived. The horse was saddled, and the young
king was all ready to mount.

Richard, when he came up to the place, assumed the command at once. He made no
obeisance to his nephew, nor did he in any other way seem to recognize or acknowledge him
as his sovereign. He simply said that he would
take care of his safety.

"The persons that have been about you,"
said he, "have been conspiring against your
life, but I will protect you."

He then ordered several of the principal of
Edward's attendants to be arrested; the rest he
commanded to disperse. What became of the
large body of men which the Earl of Rivers is

said to have had under his command does not appear. Whether they dispersed in obedience to Richard's commands, or whether they abandoned the earl and came over to Richard's side, is uncertain. At any rate, nobody resisted him. The Earl of Rivers, Lord Gray, and the others were secured, with a view of being sent off prisoners to the northward. Edward himself was to be taken with Richard back to Northampton.

The little king himself scarcely knew what to make of these proceedings. He was frightened; and when he saw that all those personal friends and attendants who had had the charge of him so long, and to whom he was strongly attached, were seized and sent away, and others, strangers to him, put in their place, he could not refrain from tears. King as he was, however, and sovereign ruler over millions of men, he was utterly helpless in his uncle's hands, and obliged to yield himself passively to the disposition which his uncle thought best to make of him.

All the accounts of Edward represent him as a kind-hearted and affectionate boy, of a gentle spirit, and of a fair and prepossessing countenance. The ancient portraits of him which remain confirm these accounts of his personal appearance and of his character.

ANCIENT PORTRAIT OF EDWARD V.

After having taken these necessary steps, and thus secured the power in his own hands, Richard vouchsafed an explanation of what he had done to the young king.   He told him that Earl Rivers, and Lord Gray, and other persons belonging to their party, "had conspired together to rule the kynge and the realme, to

sette variance among the states, and to subdue
and destroy the noble blodd of the realme,"
and that he, Richard, had interposed to save
Edward from their snares. He told him, moreover, that Lord Dorset, who was Edward's half
brother, being the son of the queen by her first
husband, and who had for some time held the
office of Chancellor of the Tower, had taken out
the king's treasure from that castle, and had
sent much of it away beyond the sea.

Edward, astonished and bewildered, did not
know at first what to reply to his uncle. He
said, however, at last, that he never heard of
any such designs on the part of his mother's
relatives, and he could not believe that the
charges were true. But Richard assured him
that they were true, and that "his kindred had
kepte their dealings from the knowledge of his
grace." Satisfied or not, Edward was silenced;
and he submitted, since it was hopeless for him
to attempt to resist, to be taken back in his uncle's custody to Northampton.

Chapter XI.

Taking Sanctuary.

WHEN the news reached London that the king had been seized on the way to the capital, and was in Gloucester's custody, it produced a universal commotion. Queen Elizabeth was thrown at once into a state of great anxiety and alarm. The tidings reached her at midnight. She was in the palace at Westminster at the time. She rose immediately in the greatest terror, and began to make preparations for fleeing to sanctuary with the Duke of York, her second son. All her friends in the neighborhood were aroused and summoned to her aid. The palace soon became a scene of universal confusion. Every body was busy packing up clothing and other necessaries in trunks and boxes, and securing jewels and valuables of various kinds, and removing them to places of safety. In the midst of this scene, the queen herself sat upon the rushes which covered the floor, half dressed, and her long and beautiful locks of hair streaming over her shoulders, the picture of despair.

There was a certain nobleman, named Lord
Hastings, who had been a very prominent and
devoted friend to Edward the Fourth during
his life, and had consequently been upon very
intimate and friendly terms with the queen. It
was he, however, that had objected in the council to the employment of a large force to conduct the young king to London, and, by so doing, had displeased the queen. Toward morning, while the queen was in the depths of her
distress and terror, making her preparations for
flight, a cheering message from Hastings was
brought to her, telling her not to be alarmed.
The message was brought to her by a certain
archbishop who had been chancellor, that is,
had had the custody of the great seal, an im-
pression from which was necessary to the validity of any royal decree. He came to deliver
up the seal to the queen, and also to bring Lord
Hastings's message.

"Ah, woe worth him !" said the queen, when
the archbishop informed her that Lord Hastings
bid her not fear. "It is he that is the cause of
all my sorrows; he goeth about to destroy me
and my blood."

"Madam," said the archbishop, "be of good
comfort. I assure you that, if they crown any
other king than your eldest son, whom they

The queen is in great distress.

have with them, we will, on the morrow, crown his brother, whom you have with you here. And here is the great seal, which, in like wise as your noble husband gave it to me, so I deliver it to you for the use of your son." So the archbishop delivered the great seal into the queen's hands, and went away. This was just before the dawn.

The words which the archbishop spoke to the queen did not give her much comfort. Indeed, her fears were not so much for her children, or for the right of the eldest to succeed to the throne, as for herself and her own personal and family ascendency under the reign of her son. She had contrived, during the lifetime of her husband, to keep pretty nearly all the influence and patronage of the government in her own hands and in that of her family connections, the Woodvilles. You will recollect how much difficulty that had made, and how strong a party had been formed against her coterie. And now, her husband being dead, what she feared was not that Gloucester, in taking the young king away from the custody of her relatives, and sending those relatives off as prisoners to the north, meant any hostility to the young king, but only against her and the whole Woodville interest, of which she was the head. She supposed that Gloucester would now put the power of the government in the hands of other families, and banish hers, and that perhaps he would even bring her to trial and punishment for acts of maladministration, or other political crimes which he would charge against her. It was fear of this, rather than any rebellion against the right of Edward the Fifth to reign, which made her in such haste to flee to sanctuary.

It was, however, somewhat uncertain what Gloucester intended to do. His professions were all very fair in respect to his allegiance to the young king. He sent a messenger to London, immediately after seizing the king, to explain his views and motives in the act, and in this communication he stated distinctly that his only object was to prevent the king's falling into the hands of the Woodville family, and not at all to oppose his coronation.

"It neyther is reason," said he in his letter, "nor in any wise to be suffered that the young kynge, our master and kinsman, should be in the hands of custody of his mother's kindred, sequestered in great measure from our companie and attendance, the which is neither honorable to hys majestie nor unto us."

Thus the pretense of Richard in seizing the king was simply that he might prevent the government under him from falling into the hands of his mother's party. But the very decisive measures he took in respect to the leading members of the Woodville family led many to suspect that he was secretly meditating a deeper design. All those who were with the king at the time of his seizure were made prisoners and sent off to a castle in the north, as we have already said; and, in order to prevent those who were in and near London from making their escape, Richard sent down immediately from Northampton ordering their arrest, and appointing guards to prevent any of them from flying to sanctuary. When the archbishop, who had called to see the queen at the palace, went away, he saw through the window, although it was yet before the dawn, a number of boats stationed on the Thames ready to intercept any who might be coming up the river with this intent from the Tower, for several influential members of the family resided at this time at the Tower.

The queen herself, however, as it happened, was at Westminster Palace, and she had accordingly but little way to go to make her escape to the Abbey.

The space which was inclosed by the consecrated limits, from within which prisoners could

9—15

not be taken, was somewhat extensive. It included not only the church of the Abbey, but also the Abbey garden, the cemetery, the palace of the abbot, the cloisters, and various other buildings and grounds included within the inclosure. As soon as the queen entered these precincts, she sank down upon the floor of the hall, " alone on the rushes, all desolate and dismayed." It was in the month of May, and the great fire-place of the hall was filled with branches of trees and flowers, while the floor, according to the custom of the time, was strewed with green rushes. For a time the queen was so overwhelmed with her sorrow and chagrin that she was scarcely conscious where she was. But she was soon aroused from her despondency by the necessity of making proper arrangements for herself and her family in her new abode. She had two daughters with her, Elizabeth and Cecily—beautiful girls, seventeen and fifteen years of age; Richard, Duke of York, her second son, and several younger children. The youngest of these children, Bridget, was only three years old. Elizabeth, the oldest, afterward became a queen, and little Bridget a nun.

The rooms which the queen and her family occupied in the sanctuary are somewhat partic-

ANCIENT VIEW OF WESTMINSTER.

ularly described by one of the writers of those days. The fire-place, where the trees and flowers were placed, was in the centre of the hall, and there was an opening in the roof above, called a *louvre*, to allow of the escape of the smoke. This hearth still remains on the floor of the hall, and the louvre is still to be seen in the roof above.* The end of the hall was formed of oak panneling, with lattice-work above, the use of which will presently appear. A part of this panneling was formed of doors, which led by winding stairs up to a curious congeries of small rooms formed among the spaces between the walls and towers, and under the arches above. Some of these rooms were for private apartments, and others were used for the offices of buttery, kitchen, laundry, and the like. At the end of this range of apartments was the private sitting-room and study of the abbot. The windows of the abbot's room looked down upon a pretty flower-garden, and there was a passage from it which led by a corridor back to the lattices over the doors in the hall, through which the abbot could look down into the hall at any time without being observed, and see what the monks were doing there.

* The room is now the college hall, so called, of Westminster school.

Besides these there were other large apartments, called state apartments, which were used chiefly on great public occasions. These rooms were larger, loftier, and more richly decorated than the others. ·They were ornamented with oak carvings and fluting, painted windows, and other such decorations. There was one in particular, which was called the Jerusalem chamber. This was the grand receiving-room of the abbot. It had a great Gothic window of painted glass, and the walls were hung with curious tapestry. This room, with the window, the tapestry, and all the other ornaments, remains to this day.

It was on the night of the third of May that the queen and her family " took sanctuary." The very next day, the fourth, was the day that the council had appointed for the coronation. But Richard, instead of coming at once to London, after taking the king under his charge, so as to be ready for the coronation at the appointed day, delayed his journey so as not to enter London until that day. He wished to prevent the coronation from taking place, having probably other plans of his own in view instead.

It is not, however, absolutely certain that Richard intended, at this time, to claim the crown for himself, for in entering London he

formed a grand procession, giving the young
king the place of honor in it, and doing homage to him as king. Richard himself and all
his retinue were in mourning. Edward was
dressed in a royal mantle of purple velvet, and
rode conspicuously as the chief personage of
the procession. A short distance from the city
the cavalcade was met by a procession of the
civic authorities of London and five hundred
citizens, all sumptuously appareled, who had
come out to receive and welcome their sovereign, and to conduct him through the gates into
the city. In entering the city Richard rode immediately before the king, with his head uncov-
ered. He held his cap in his hand, and bowed
continually very low before the king, designating him in this way to the citizens as the object of their homage. He called out also, from
time to time, to the crowds that thronged the
waysides to see, "Behold your prince and sovereign."

There were two places to which it might
have been considered not improbable that Richard would take the king on his arrival at the
capital—one the palace of Westminster, at the
upper end of London, and the other the Tower,
at the lower end. The Tower, though often
used as a prison, was really, at that time, a

castle, where the kings and the members of the
royal family often resided. Richard, however,
did not go to either of these places at first, but
proceeded instead to the bishop's palace at St.
Paul's, in the heart of the city. Here a sort of
court was established, a grand council of nobles
and officers of state was called, and for some
days the laws were administered and the government was carried on from this place, all,
however, in Edward's name. Money was coin-
ed, also, with his effigy and inscription, and, in
fine, so far as all essential forms and technicali-
ties were concerned, the young Edward was
really a reigning king; but, of course, in respect
to substantial power, every thing was in Richard's hands.

The reason why Richard did not proceed at
once to the Tower was probably because Dorset, the queen's son, was in command there,
and he, as of course he was identified with the
Woodville party, might perhaps have made
Richard some trouble. But Dorset, as soon as
he heard that Richard was coming, abandoned
the Tower, and fled to the sanctuary to join his
mother. Accordingly, after waiting a few days
at the bishop's palace until the proper arrangements could be made, the king, with the whole
party in attendance upon him, removed to the

Tower, and took up their residence there. The
king was nominally in his castle, with Richard
and the other nobles and their retinue in attendance upon him as his guards. Really he
was in a prison, and his uncle, with the people
around him who were under his uncle's command, were his keepers.

A meeting of the lords was convened, and
various political arrangements were made to
suit Richard's views. The principal members
of the Woodville family were dismissed from
the offices which they held, and other nobles,
who were in Richard's interest, were appointed
in their place. A new day was appointed for
the coronation, namely, the 22d of June. The
council of lords decreed also that, as the king
was yet too young to conduct the government
himself personally, his uncle Gloucester was,
for the present, to have charge of the adminis-
tration of public affairs, under the title of Lord
Protector. The title in full, which Richard
thenceforth assumed under this decree, was,
Richard, Duke of Gloucester, brother and uncle
of the king, Protector and Defender, Great
Chamberlain, Constable, and Lord High Admiral of England.

During all this time the city of London, and,
indeed, the whole realm of England, as far as

the tidings of what was going on at the capital
spread into the interior, had been in a state of
the greatest excitement. The nobles, and the
courtiers of all ranks, were constantly on the
alert, full of anxiety and solicitude, not know-
ing which side to take or what sentiments to
avow. They did not know what turn things
would finally take, and, of course, could not tell
what they were to do in order to be found, in
the end, on the side that was uppermost. The
common people in the streets, with anxious
looks and many fearful forebodings, discussed
the reports and rumors that they had heard.
They all felt a sentiment of loyal and affectionate regard for the king—a sentiment which was
increased and strengthened by his youth, his
gentle disposition, and the critical and helpless
situation that he was in; while, on the other
hand, the character of Gloucester inspired them
with a species of awe which silenced and subdued them. Edward, in his "protector's" hands,
seemed to them like a lamb in the custody of
a tiger.

The queen, all this time, remained shut up
in the sanctuary, in a state of extreme suspense
and anxiety, clinging to the children whom she
had with her, and especially to her youngest
son, the little Duke of York, as the next heir to

Forlorn situation of the queen.

THE PEOPLE IN THE STREETS.

the crown, and her only stay and hope, in case,
through Richard's violence or treachery, any
calamity should befall the king.

CHAPTER XII.

RICHARD LORD PROTECTOR.

WHAT sort of protection Richard afforded to the young wards who were committed to his charge will appear by events narrated in this chapter.

It was now June, and the day, the twenty-second, which had been fixed upon for the coronation, was drawing nigh. By the ancient usages of the realm of England, the office of Protector, to which Richard had been appointed, would expire on the coronation of the king. Of course, Richard perceived at once that if he wished to prolong his power he must act promptly.

He began to revolve in his mind the possibility of assuming the crown himself, and displacing the children of his older brothers; for Clarence left children at his decease as well as Edward. Of course, these children of Clarence, as well as those of Edward, would take precedence of him in the line of succession, being descended from an older brother. Richard therefore, in order to establish any claim to the crown for himself,

His plan for disposing of Edward's children.

CLARENCE'S CHILDREN HEARING OF THEIR FATHER'S DEATH.

must find some pretext for setting aside both these branches of the family. The pretexts which he found were these.

In respect to the children of Edward, his plan was to pretend to have discovered proof of Edward's having been privately married to another lady before his marriage with Elizabeth

Woodville. This would, of course, render the marriage with Elizabeth Woodville null, and destroy the rights of the children to any inheritance from their father.

In respect to the children of Clarence, he was to maintain that they were cut off by the attainder which had been passed against their father. A bill of attainder, according to the laws and usages of those times, not only doomed the criminal himself to death, but cut off his children from all rights of inheritance. It was intended to destroy the family as well as the man.

Richard, however, did not at once reveal his plans, but proceeded cautiously to take the proper measures for putting them into execution.

In the first place, there was his mother to be conciliated, the Lady Cecily Neville, known, however, more generally by the title of the Duchess of York. She lived at this time in an old family residence called Baynard's Castle, which stood on the banks of the Thames.* As soon as Richard arrived in London he went to see his mother at this place, and afterward he often visited her there. How far he explained his plans to her, and how far she encouraged or disapproved of them, is not known. If she was

* For a view of this castle, see engraving on page 273.

required to act at all in the case, it must have been very hard for her, in such a question of life and death, to decide between her youngest son alive and the children of her first-born in his grave. Mothers can best judge to which side, in such an alternative, her maternal sympathies would naturally incline her.

As for the immediate members of the Woodville family, they were already pretty well taken care of. The queen herself, with her children, were shut up in the sanctuary. Her brothers, and the other influential men who were most prominent on her side, had been made prisoners, and sent to Pomfret Castle in the north. Here they were held under the custody of men devoted to Richard's interest. But to prevent the possibility of his having any farther trouble with them, Richard resolved to order them to be beheaded. This resolution was soon carried into effect, as we shall presently see.

There remained the party of nobles and courtiers that were likely to be hostile to the permanent continuance of the power of Richard, and inclined to espouse the cause of the young king. The nobles had not yet distinctly taken ground on this question. There were, however, some who were friendly to Richard. Others seemed more inclined to form a party against him. The prominent man among this last-named set was Lord Hastings. There were several others besides, and Richard knew very well who they were. In order to circumvent and defeat any plans which they might be disposed to form, and to keep the power fully in his own hands, he convened his councils of state at different places, sometimes at Westminster, sometimes at the Tower, where the king was kept, and sometimes at his own residence, which was in the heart of London. He transferred the public business more and more to his own residence, assembling the councilors there at all times, late and early, and thus withdrawing them from attendance at the Tower. Very soon Richard's residence in London became the acknowledged head-quarters of influence and power, and all who had petitions to present or favors to obtain gathered there, while the king in the Tower was neglected, and left comparatively alone.

Still the form of holding a council from time to time at the Tower was continued, and, of course, the nobles who assembled there were those most inclined to stand by and defend the cause of the king.

Such was the state of things on the 13th of June, nine days before the time appointed for the coronation. Richard then, having carefully laid his plans, was prepared to take decisive measures to break up the party who were disposed to gather around the king at the Tower and espouse his cause.

On that day, while these nobles were holding a council in the Tower, suddenly, and greatly to their surprise, Richard walked in among them. He assumed a very good-natured and even merry air as he entered and took his seat, and began to talk with those present in a very friendly and familiar tone. This was for the purpose of lulling any suspicions which they might have felt on seeing him appear among them, and prevent them from divining the dreadful intentions with which he had come.

"My lord," said he, turning to a bishop who sat near him, and who was one of those that he was about to arrest, " you have some excellent strawberries in your garden, I understand. I wish you would let me have a plateful of them."

It was about the middle of June, you will recollect, which was the time for strawberries to be ripe.

The bishop was very much pleased to find the great Protector taking such an interest in his strawberries, and he immediately called a

9—16

servant and sent him away at once to bring
some of the fruit.

After having greeted the other nobles at the
board in a somewhat similar style to this, with
jocose and playful remarks, which had the effect of entirely diverting from their minds every
thing like suspicion, he said that he must go
away for a short time, but that he would presently return. In the mean time, they might
proceed, he said, with their deliberations on the
public business.

So he went out. He proceeded at once to
make the preparations necessary for the accomplishment of the desperate measures which he
had determined to adopt. He stationed armed
men at the doors and the passages of the part
of the Tower where the council was assembled,
and gave them instructions as to what they
were to do, and agreed with them in respect to
the signals which he was to give.

In about an hour he returned, but his whole
air and manner were now totally changed. He
came in with a frowning and angry countenance, knitting his brows and setting his teeth,
as if something had occurred to put him in a
great rage. He advanced to the council table,
and there accosting Lord Hastings in a very
excited and angry manner, he demanded,

"What punishment do you think men deserve who form plots and schemes for my destruction?"

Lord Hastings was amazed at this sudden appearance of displeasure, and he replied to the Protector that such men, if there were any such, most certainly deserved death, whoever they might be.

"It is that sorceress, my brother's wife," said Richard, "and that other vile sorceress, worse than she, Jane Shore. See!"

This allusion to Jane Shore was somewhat ominous for Hastings, as it was generally understood that since the king's death Lord Hastings had taken Jane Shore under his protection, and had lived in great intimacy with her.

As Richard said this, he pulled up the sleeve of his doublet to the elbow, to let the company look at his arm. This arm had always been weak, and smaller than the other.

"See," said he, "what they are doing to me."

He meant that by the power of necromancy they had made an image of wax as an effigy of him, according to the mode explained in a previous chapter, and were now melting it away by slow degrees in order to destroy his life, and that his arm was beginning to pine and wither away in consequence.

16

Scene in the council chamber at the Tower.

THE COUNCIL IN THE TOWER.

The lords knew very well that the state in which they saw Richard's arm was its natural condition, and that, consequently, his charge against the queen and Jane Shore was only a pretense, which was to be the prelude and excuse for some violent measures that he was about to take. They scarcely knew what to say. At last Lord Hastings replied,

"Certainly, my lord, if they have committed so heinous an offense as this, they deserve a very heinous punishment."

"If!" repeated the Protector, in a voice of

He makes signals for the armed men to come in.

thunder. "And thou servest me, then, it seems, with *ifs* and *ands*. I tell thee that they *have* so done—and I will make what I say good upon thy body, traitor!"

He emphasized and confirmed this threat by bringing down his fist with a furious blow upon the table.

This was one of the signals which he had agreed upon with the people that he had stationed without at the door of the council hall. A voice was immediately heard in the antechamber calling out Treason. This was again another signal. It was a call to a band of armed men whom Richard had stationed in a convenient place near by, and who were to rush in at this call. Accordingly, a sudden noise was heard of the rushing of men and the clanking of iron, and before the councilors could recover from their consternation the table was surrounded with soldiery, all "in harness," that is, completely armed, and as fast as the foremost came in and gathered around the table, others pressed in after them, until the room was completely full.

Richard, designating Hastings with a gesture, said suddenly, "I arrest thee, traitor."

"What! *me*, my lord?" exclaimed Hastings, in terror.

"Yes, thee, traitor."

Two or three of the soldiers immediately
seized Hastings and prepared to lead him
away. Other soldiers laid hands upon several
of the other nobles, such as Richard had designated to them beforehand. These, of course,
were the leading and prominent men of the
party opposed to Richard's permanent ascendency. Most of these men were taken away and
secured as prisoners in various parts of the
Tower. As for Hastings, Richard, in a stern
and angry manner, advised him to lose no time
in saying his prayers, "for, by the Lord," said
he, "I will not to dinner to-day till I see thy
head off."

Then, after a brief delay, to allow the wretched man a few minutes to say his prayers, Richard nodded to the soldiers to signify to them
that they were to proceed to their work. They
immediately took their victim out to a green
by the side of the Tower, and, laying him down
with his neck across a log which they found
there, they cut off his head with a broad-axe.

The same day Richard sent off a dispatch to
the north, directed to the men who had in
charge the Earl Rivers, and the other friends of
the king who had been made prisoners when
the king was seized at Stony Stratford, order-

POMFRET CASTLE

ing them all to be beheaded. The order was immediately obeyed.

The person who had charge of the execution of this order was a stern and ruffian-like officer named Sir Richard Ratcliffe. This man is quite noted in the history of the times as one of the most unscrupulous of Richard's adherents. He was a merciless man, short and rude in speech, and reckless in action, destitute alike of all pity for man and of all fear of God.

The place where the prisoners had been confined was Pomfret Castle.* On receiving the orders from Richard, Ratcliffe led them out to an open place without the castle wall to be beheaded. The executioners brought a log and an axe, and the victims were slaughtered one after another, without any ceremony, and without being allowed to say a word in self-defense.

The whole country was shocked at hearing of these sudden and terrible executions; but the power was in Richard's hands, and there was no one capable of resisting him. The death of the leaders of what would have been the young king's party struck terror into the rest, and Richard now had every thing in his own hands, or, rather, *almost* every thing; for the queen and her family, being still in the sanctuary,

* Called sometimes Pontefract.

were beyond his reach. He, however, had nothing to fear from her personally, and there were
none of the children that gave him any concern
except the Duke of York, the king's younger
brother. He, you will recollect, was with his
mother at Westminster when the king was
seized, and she had taken him with the other
children to the Abbey. Richard was now extremely desirous of getting possession of this
boy.

The reason why he deemed it so essential to
get possession of him was this. The child was,
it is true, of little consequence while his brother the king lived; but if the king were put
out of the way, then the thoughts and the hearts
of all the loyal people of England, Richard
knew very well, would be turned toward York
as the rightful successor. But if they could
both be put out of the way, and if the people
of England could be induced to consider Clarence's children as set aside by the attainder of
their father, then he himself would come forward as the true and rightful heir to the crown.
It is true that it was a part of his plan, as has
already been said, to declare the marriage of
Elizabeth Woodville with the king null, and
thus cut off both these children of Edward from
their right of inheritance; but he knew very

He determines to seize him.

well that even if a majority of the people of
England were to assent to this, there would certainly be a minority that would refuse their assent, and would adhere to the cause of the children, and they, if the children should fall into
their hands, might, at some future time, make
themselves very formidable to him, and threat-
en very seriously the permanence of his do-
minion. It was quite necessary, therefore, he
thought, that he should get both children into
his own power.

"I must," said he to himself, therefore, "I
must, in some way or other, and at all hazards,
get possession of little Richard."

It is always the policy of usurpers, and of all
ambitious and aspiring men who wish to seize
and hold power which does not properly belong
to them, to carry the various measures necessary to the attainment of their ends, especially
those likely to be unpopular, not by their own
personal action, but by the agency of others,
whom they put forward to act for them. Richard proceeded in this way in the present instance. He called a grand council of the peers
of the realm and great officers of state, and
caused the question to be brought up there of
removing the young Duke of York from the
custody of his mother to that of the Protector,

in order that he might be with his brother. The peers who were in Richard's interest advocated this plan; but all the bishops and archbishops, who, of course, as ecclesiastics, had very high ideas of the sacredness and inviolability of a sanctuary, opposed the plan of taking the duke away except by the consent of his mother.

The other side argued in reply to them that a sanctuary was a place where persons could seek refuge to escape punishment in case of crime, and that where no crime could have been committed, and no charges of crime were made, the principle did not apply. In other words, that the sanctuary was for men and women who had been guilty, or were supposed to have been guilty, of violations of law; but as children could commit no crime for which an asylum was necessary, the privileges of sanctuary did not extend to them.

This view of the subject prevailed. The bishops and archbishops were outvoted, and an order in council was passed authorizing the Lord Protector to possess himself of his nephew, the Duke of York, and for this purpose to take him, if necessary, out of sanctuary by force.

Still, the bishops and archbishops were very unwilling that force should be used, if it could possibly be avoided; and finally the Archbish·

op of Canterbury, who was the highest prelate in the realm, proposed that a deputation from the council should be sent to the Abbey, and that he should go with them, in order to see the queen, and make the attempt to persuade her to give up her son of her own accord.

After giving notice to the abbot of their intended visit, and making an arrangement with him and with the queen in respect to the time when they could be received, the delegation proceeded in state to the Abbey on the appointed day, and were received by the abbot and by Elizabeth with due ceremony in the Jerusalem chamber, the great audience hall of the Abbey, which has already been described.

The Archbishop of Canterbury, who was at the head of the delegation, explained the case to the queen. They wished her, he said, to allow her son, the Duke of York, to leave the sanctuary, and to join his brother the king at his royal residence in the Tower. He would be perfectly safe there, he said, under the care of his uncle, the Lord Protector.

"The Protector thinks it very necessary that the duke should go," added the archbishop, "to be company for his brother. The king is very melancholy, he says, for want of a play-fellow."

" And so the Protector," replied the queen—
"God grant that he may really prove a protector—thinks that the king needs a playfellow ! And can no playfellow be found for him
except his brother ?

"Besides," she added, "he is not in a mood
to play. He is not well. They must find some
other playmate for his brother. Just as if
princes, while they are so young, could not as
well have some one to play with them not of
their own rank, or as if a boy must have his
brother, and nobody else for his mate, when
every body knows that boys are more likely
to disagree with their brothers than they are
with other children."

The archbishop, in reply, proceeded to argue
the case with the queen, and to represent the
necessity, arising from reasons of state, why the
young duke should be committed to the charge
of his uncle. He explained to her, too, that the
Lord Protector had been fully authorized, by a
decree of the council, to come and take his
nephew from the Abbey, and to employ force, if
necessary, to effect the purpose, but that it would
be much better, both for the queen herself and
the young duke, as well as for all concerned,
that the affair should be settled in a peaceable
and amicable manner.

The unhappy queen saw at last that there was no alternative but for her to submit to her fate and give up her boy. Slowly and reluctantly she came to this conclusion, and finally gave her consent. Richard was brought in. His mother took him by the hand, and again addressed the archbishop and the delegation, speaking substantially as follows:

"My lord," said she, "and all my lords now present, I will not be so suspicious as to mistrust the promises you make me, or to believe that you are dealing otherwise than fairly and honorably by me. Here is my son. I give him up to your charge. I have no doubt that he would be safe here under my protection, if I could be allowed to keep him with me, although I have enemies that so hate me and all my blood, that I believe, if they thought they had any of it in their own veins, they would open them to let it flow out.

"I give him up, at your demand, to the protection of his brother and his uncle. And yet I know well that the desire of a kingdom knows no kindred. Brothers have been their brothers' bane, and can these nephews be sure of their uncle? The boys would be safe if kept asunder; together—I do not know. Nevertheless, I here deliver my son, and with him his broth-

er's life, into your hands, and of you shall I require them both, before God and man. I know
that you are faithful and true in what you intend, and you have power, moreover, to keep
the children safe, if you will. If you think that
I am over-anxious and fear too much, take care
that you yourselves do not fear too little."

Then drawing Richard to her, she kissed him
very lovingly, the tears coming to her eyes as
she did so.

"Farewell," she said, "farewell, mine own
sweet son. God send you good keeping. I
must kiss you before you go, for God knows
when we shall kiss together again."

She kissed him again and blessed him, and
then turned to go away, weeping bitterly.

The child began to weep too, from sympathy
with his mother's distress. The archbishop,
however, took him by the hand and led him
away, followed by the rest of the delegation.

They conveyed the young duke first to the
hall of the council, which was very near, and
thence to the Lord Protector's residence in the
city. Here he was received with every mark
of consideration and honor, and a handsome escort was provided to conduct him in state to
the Tower, where he joined his brother.

Richard had now every thing under his own

Both princes entirely in Richard's power.

control. The delivery of the Duke of York into his hands took place on the sixteenth of June. The time which had been set for the coronation was the twenty-second.

9—17

CHAPTER XIII.
PROCLAIMED KING.

RICHARD, having thus obtained control of every thing essential to the success of his plans, began to prepare for action. His chief friend and confederate, the one on whom he relied most for the execution of the several measures which he proposed to take, was a powerful nobleman named the Duke of Buckingham. I shall proceed in this chapter to describe the successive steps of the course which Richard and the Duke of Buckingham pursued in raising Richard to the throne, as recorded by the different historians of those days, and as generally believed since, though, in fact, there have been great disputes in respect to these occurrences, and it is now quite difficult to ascertain with certainty what the precise truth of the case really is. This, however, is, after all, of no great practical importance, for, in respect to remote transactions of this nature, the thing which is most necessary for the purposes of general education is to understand what the story is, in detail, which has been generally received among mankind, and to which the allusions of orators and poets, and the discussions of statesmen and moralists in subsequent ages refer, for it is with this story alone that for all the purposes of general reading we have any thing to do.

Richard was residing at this time chiefly at Baynard's Castle with his mother.* The young king and his brother, the Duke of York, were in the Tower. They were not nominally prisoners, but yet Richard kept close watch and ward over them, and took most effectual precautions to prevent their making their escape. The queen, Elizabeth Woodville, with her daughters, was in the sanctuary. Richard's wife, with the young child, was still at Middleham Castle.

It is a very curious circumstance, showing how sometimes records of the most trivial and insignificant things come down to us from ancient times in a clear and certain form, while all that is really important to know is involved in doubt and obscurity—that the household expense-book of Anne at Middleham is still extant, showing all the little items of expense incurred for Richard's son, while all is dispute and uncertainty in respect to the great political

* For view of this castle, see page 273.

17

schemes and measures of his father. In this book there is a charge of 22s. 9d. for a piece of green cloth, and another of 1s. 8d. for making it into gowns for "my lord prince." There is also a charge of 5s. for a feather for him, and 13s. 1d. paid to a shoemaker, named Dirick, for a pair of shoes. This expense-book was continued after Anne left Middleham Castle to go to London, as will be presently related. There are several charges on the journey for offerings and gifts made by the child at churches on the way. Two men were paid 6s. 8d. for running on foot by the side of his carriage. These men's names were Medcalf and Pacock. There is also a charge of 2d. for mending a whip!

But to return to our narrative. The time for the coronation of Edward the Fifth was drawing near, but Richard intended to prevent the performance of this ceremony, and to take the crown for himself instead. The first thing was to put in circulation the story that his two nephews were not the legitimate children of his brother, Edward the Fourth, and to prepare the way for this, he wished first, by every means, to cast odium on Edward's character. This was easily done, for Edward's character was bad enough to merit any degree of odium which his brother might wish it to bear.

Accordingly, Richard employed his friends and partisans in talking as much as possible in all quarters about the dissoluteness and the vices of the late king. False stories would probably have been invented, if it had not been that there were enough that were true. These stories were all revived and put in circulation, and every thing was made to appear as unfavorable for Edward as possible. Richard himself, on the other hand, feigned a very strict and scrupulous regard for virtue and morality, and deemed it his duty, he said, to do all in his power to atone for and wipe away the reproach which his brother's loose and wicked life had left upon the court and the kingdom. Among other things, the cause of public morals demanded, he said, that an example should be made of Jane Shore, who had been the associate and partner of the king in his immoralities.

Jane Shore, it will be recollected, was the wife of a rich citizen of London, whom Edward had enticed away from her husband and brought to court. She was naturally a very amiable and kind-hearted woman, and all accounts concur in saying that she exercised the power that she acquired over the mind of the king in a very humane and praiseworthy manner. She was always ready to interpose, when the king

contemplated any act of harshness or severity,
to avert his anger and save his intended victim,
and, in general, she did a great deal to soften
the brutality of his character, and to protect the
innocent and helpless from the wrongs which
he would otherwise have often done them.
These amiable and gentle traits of character do
not, indeed, atone at all for the grievous sin
which she committed in abandoning her husband and living voluntarily with the king, but
they did much toward modifying the feeling of
scorn and contempt with which she would have
otherwise been regarded by the people of England.

Richard caused Jane to be arrested and sent
to prison.   He also seized all her plate and jewels, and confiscated them.   She had a very rich
and valuable collection of these things.*   Richard then caused an ecclesiastical court to be organized, and sent her before it to be tried.   The
court, undoubtedly in accordance with instructions that Richard himself gave them, sentenced
her, by way of penance for her sins, to walk in
midday through the streets of London, from
one end of the city to the other, almost entirely

---

* The husband with whom she had lived before she became acquainted with Edward was a wealthy goldsmith ◦
and jeweler.

The punishment of Jane Shore.

undressed.   The intention of this severe expo-
sure was to designate her to those who should
assemble to witness the punishment as a wan-
ton, and thus to put her to shame, and draw
upon her the scorn and derision of the populace.   They found some old and obsolete law
which authorized such a punishment.   The
sentence was carried into effect on a Sunday.
The unhappy criminal was conducted through
the principal streets of the city, wearing a night-
dress, and carrying a lighted taper in her hand,
between rows of spectators that assembled by
thousands along the way to witness the scene.
But, instead of being disposed to receive her
with taunts and reproaches, the populace were
moved to compassion by her saddened look and
her extreme beauty.   Their hearts were soft-
ened by the remembrance of the many stories
they had heard of the kindness of her heart,
and the amiableness and gentleness of her de-
meanor, in the time of her prosperity and power.   They thought it hard, too, that the law
should be enforced so rigidly against her alone,
while so many multitudes in all ranks of society, high as well as low, were allowed to go
unpunished.

Still, Richard's object in this exhibition was
accomplished.   The transaction had the effect

Alleged marriage of Edward IV. to Elinor Talbot.

of calling the attention of the public universally and strongly to the fact that Edward the Fourth had been a loose and dissolute man, and prepared people's minds for the charge which was about to be brought against him.

This charge was that he had been secretly married to another lady before his union with Elizabeth Woodville, and that consequently by this latter marriage he was guilty of bigamy. Of course, if this were true, the second marriage would be null and void, and the children springing from it would have no rights as heirs.

Whether there was any truth in this story or not can not now ever be certainly known. All that is certain is that Richard circulated the report, and he found several witnesses to testify to the truth of it. The maiden name of the lady to whom they said the king had been married was Elinor Talbot. She had married in early life a certain Lord Boteler, whose widow she was at the time that Edward was alleged to have married her. The marriage was performed in a very private manner by a certain bishop, nobody being present besides the parties except the bishop himself, and he was strictly charged by the king to keep the affair a profound secret. This he promised to do. Notwithstanding his promise, however, the bishop some time subsequently, after the king had been married to Elizabeth Woodville, revealed the secret of the previous marriage to Gloucester, at which the king, when he heard of it, was extremely angry. He accused the bishop of having betrayed the trust which he had reposed in him, and, dismissing him at once from office, shut him up in prison.

Richard having, as he said, kept these facts secret during his brother's lifetime, out of regard for the peace of the family, now felt it his duty to make them known, in order to prevent the wrong which would be done by allowing the crown to descend to a son who, not being born in lawful wedlock, could have no rights as heir.

After disseminating this story among the influential persons connected with the court, and through all the circles of high life, during the week, it was arranged that on the following Sunday the facts should be made known publicly to the people.

There was a large open space near St. Paul's Cathedral, in the very heart of London, where it was the custom to hold public assemblies of all kinds, both religious and political. There was a pulpit built on one side of this space, from which sermons were preached, orations

Sermon preached by Dr. Shaw near St. Paul's.

and harangues pronounced, and proclamations made. Oaths were administered here too, in cases where it was required to administer oaths to large numbers of people.

From this pulpit, on the next Sunday after the penance of Jane Shore, a certain Dr. Shaw, who was a brother of the Lord-mayor of London, preached a sermon to a large concourse of citizens, in which he openly attempted to set aside the claims of the two boys, and to prove that Richard was the true heir to the crown.

He took for his text a passage from the Wisdom of Solomon, "The multiplying brood of the ungodly shall not thrive." In this discourse he explained to his audience that Edward, when he was married to Elizabeth Woodville, was already the husband of Elinor Boteler, and consequently that the second marriage was illegal and void, and the children of it entirely destitute of all claims to the crown. He also, it is said, advanced the idea that neither Edward nor Clarence were the children of their reputed father, the old Duke of York, but that Richard was the oldest legitimate son of the marriage, in proof of which he offered the fact that Richard strongly resembled the duke in person, while neither Edward nor Clarence had borne any resemblance to him at all.

It was arranged, moreover—so it was said—
that, when the preacher came to the passage
where he was to speak of the resemblance
which Richard bore to his father, the great Duke
of York, Richard himself was to enter the assembly as if by accident, and thus give the
preacher the opportunity to illustrate and confirm what he had said by directing his audience to observe for themselves the resemblance which he had pointed out, and also to
excite them to a burst of enthusiasm in Richard's favor by the eloquent appeal which the
incident of Richard's entrance was to awaken.
But this intended piece of stage effect, if it was
really planned, failed in the execution. Richard did not come in at the right time, and when
he did come in, either the preacher managed
the case badly, or else the people were very little disposed to espouse Richard's cause; for
when the orator, at the close of his appeal, expected applause and acclamations, the people
uttered no response, but looked at each other in
silence, and remained wholly unmoved.

In the course of the following two or three
days, other attempts were made to excite the
populace to some demonstration in Richard's
favor, but they did not succeed. The Duke of
Buckingham met a large concourse of London-

ers at the Guildhall, which is in the centre of
the business portion of the city. He was sup-
ported by a number of nobles, knights, and distinguished citizens, and he made a long and
able speech to the assembly, in which he argued
strenuously in favor of calling Richard to the
throne. He denounced the character of the former king, and enlarged at length on the dissi-
pated and vicious life which he had led. He
also related to the people the story of Edward's
having been the husband of Lady Elinor Boteler
at the time when his marriage with Queen Elizabeth took place, which fact, as Buckingham
showed, made the marriage with Elizabeth
void, and cut off the children from the inheritance. The children of Clarence had been cut
off, too, by the attainder, and so Richard was the
only remaining heir.

The duke concluded his harangue by asking
the assembly if, under those circumstances, they
would not call upon Richard to ascend the
throne. A few of the poorer sort, very likely
some that had been previously hired to do it,
threw up their caps into the air in response to
this appeal, and cried out, "Long live King
Richard!" But the major part, comprising all
the more respectable portion of the assembly,
looked grave and were silent. Some who were

pressed to give their opinion said they must take time to consider.

Thus these appeals to the people failed, so far as the object of them was to call forth a popular demonstration in Richard's favor. But in one respect they accomplished the object in view: they had the effect of making it known throughout London and the vicinity that a revolution was impending, and thus preparing men's minds to acquiesce in the change more readily than they might perhaps have done if it had come upon them suddenly and with a shock.

On the following day after the address at the Guildhall, a grand assembly of all the lords, bishops, councilors, and officers of state was convened in Westminster. It was substantially a Parliament, though not a Parliament in form. The reason why it was not called as a Parliament in form was because Richard, having doubts, as he said, about the right of Edward to the throne, could not conscientiously advise that any public act should be performed in his name; and a Parliament could only be legally convened by summons from a king. Accordingly, this assembly was only an informal meeting of the peers of England and other great dignitaries of Church and State, with a view of consulting

together to determine what should be done.
Of course, it was all fully arranged and settled
beforehand, among those who were in Richard's
confidence, what the result of these deliberations was to be. The Duke of Buckingham,
Richard's principal friend and supporter, managed the business at the meeting. The assembly consisted, of course, chiefly of the party of
Richard's friends. The principal leaders of the
parties opposed to him had been beheaded or
shut up in prison; of the rest, some had fled,
some had concealed themselves, and of the few
who dared to show themselves at the meeting,
there were none who had the courage, or perhaps I ought rather to say the imprudence and
folly, to oppose any thing which Buckingham
should undertake to do.

The result of the deliberations of this council
was the drawing up of a petition to be presented to Richard, declaring him the true and rightful heir to the crown, and praying him to assume at once the sovereign power.

A delegation was appointed to wait upon
Richard and present the petition to him. Buckingham was at the head of this delegation. The
petition was written out in due form upon a roll
of parchment. It declared that, inasmuch as it
was clearly established that King Edward the

Fourth was already the husband of "Dame Ali-
onora Boteler," by a previous marriage, at the
time of his pretended marriage with Elizabeth
Woodville, and that consequently his children
by Elizabeth Woodville, not being born in lawful wedlock, could have no rights of inheritance
whatever from their father, and especially could
by no means derive from him any title to the
crown; and inasmuch as the children of Clarence had been cut off from the succession by
the bill of attainder which had been passed
against their father; and inasmuch as Richard
came next in order to these in the line of succession, therefore he was now the true and
rightful heir. This his right moreover by birth
was now confirmed by the decision of the estates of the realm assembled for the purpose;
wherefore the petition, in conclusion, invited
and urged him at once to assume the crown
which was thus his by a double title—the right
of birth and the election of the three estates of
the realm.

Of course, although the petition was addressed to Richard as if the object of it was to produce an effect upon his mind, it was really all
planned and arranged by Richard himself, and
by Buckingham in conjunction with him; and
the representations and arguments which it

contained were designed solely for effect on the
mind of the public, when the details of the
transaction should be promulgated throughout
the land.

The petition being ready, Buckingham, in be-
half of the delegation, demanded an audience
of the Lord Protector that they might lay it
before him.   Richard accordingly made an ap-
pointment to receive them at his mother's residence at Baynard's Castle.

At the appointed time the delegation appeared, and were received in great state by Richard
in the audience hall.   The Duke of Buckingham presented the petition, and Richard read
it.   He seemed surprised, and he pretended to
be at a loss what to reply.   Presently he began
to say that he could not think of assuming the
crown.   He said he had no ambition to reign,
but only desired to preserve the kingdom for
his nephew the king until he should become
of sufficient age, and then to put him peaceably
in possession of it.   But the Duke of Buckingham replied that this could never be.   The people of England, he said, would never consent to
be ruled by a prince of illegitimate birth.

" And if you, my lord," added the duke, " refuse to accept the crown, they know where to
find another who will gladly accept it."

BAYNARD'S CASTLE.

9—18

In the end, Richard allowed himself to be
persuaded that there was no alternative but for
him to accept the crown, and he reluctantly
consented that, on the morrow, he would proceed in state to Westminster, and publicly assume the title and the prerogatives of king.

Accordingly, the next day, a grand procession was formed, and Richard was conducted
with great pomp to Westminster Hall.   Here
he took his place on the throne, with the leading lords of his future court, and the bishops
and archbishops around him.   The rest of the
hall was crowded with a vast concourse of people that had assembled to witness the ceremony.

First the king took the customary royal oath,
which was administered by the archbishop.
He then summoned the great judges before
him, and made an address to them, exhorting
them to administer the laws and execute judgment between man and man in a just and im-
partial manner, inasmuch as to secure that end,
he said, would be the first and greatest object
of his reign.

After this Richard addressed the concourse
of people in the hall, who, in some sense, represented the public, and pronounced a pardon for
all offenses which had been committed against
himself, and ordered a proclamation to be made

of a general amnesty throughout the land. These announcements were received by the people with loud acclamations, and the ceremony was concluded by shouts of "Long live King Richard!" from all the assembly.

We obtain a good idea of this scene by the following engraving, which is copied exactly from a picture contained in a manuscript volume of the time.

THE KING ON HIS THRONE.

The royal dignity having thus been assumed by the new king at the usual centre and seat of the royal power, the procession was again formed, and Richard was conducted to Westminster Abbey for the purpose of doing the homage customary on such occasions at one of the shrines in the church. The procession of the king was met at the door of the church by a procession of monks chanting a solemn anthem as they came.

After the religious ceremonies were completed, Richard, at the head of a grand cavalcade of knights, noblemen, and citizens, proceeded into the city to the Church of St. Paul. The streets were lined with spectators, who saluted the king with cheers and acclamations as he passed. At the Church of St. Paul more ceremonies were performed and more proclamations were made. The popular joy, more or less sincere, was expressed by the sounding of trumpets, the waving of banners, and loud acclamations of "Long live King Richard!" At length, when the services in the city were concluded, the king returned to Westminster, and took up his abode at the royal palace; and while he was returning, heralds were sent to all the great centres of concourse and intelligence in and around London to proclaim him king.

This proclamation of Richard as king took place on the twenty-sixth of June. King Ed-

ward the Fourth died just about three months
before.   During this three months Edward the
Fifth is, in theory, considered as having been
the King of England, though, during the whole
period, the poor child, instead of exercising any
kingly rights or prerogatives, was a helpless
prisoner in the hands of others, who, while they
professed to be his protectors, were really his
determined and relentless foes.

A.D. 1483.] THE CORONATION. 279

Plan for the coronation.   Anne is sent for, and comes to London.

CHAPTER XIV.

THE CORONATION.

IT was on the 26th of June, 1483, that Richard was proclaimed king, under the circumstances narrated in the last chapter. In order to render his investiture with the royal authority complete, he resolved that the ceremony of coronation should be immediately performed. He accordingly appointed the 6th of July for the day. This allowed an interval of just ten days for the necessary preparations.

The first thing to be done was to send to Middleham Castle for Anne, his wife, who now, since the proclamation of Richard, became Queen of England. Richard wished that she should be present, and take part in the ceremony of the coronation. The child was to be brought too. His name was Edward.

It seems that Anne arrived in London only on the 3d of July, three days before the appointed day. There is a specification in the book of accounts of some very elegant and costly cloth of gold bought on that day in London, the material for the queen's coronation robe.

Richard determined that the ceremony of his coronation should be more magnificent than that of any previous English monarch. Preparations were made, accordingly, on a very grand scale. There were several preliminary pageants and processions on the days preceding that of the grand ceremony.

On the 4th of July, which was Sunday, the king and queen proceeded in state to the Tower. They went in barges on the river. The party set out from Baynard's Castle, the residence of Richard's mother, and the place where the queen went on her arrival in London.

The royal barges destined to convey the king and queen, and the other great personages of the party, were covered with canopies of silk, and were otherwise magnificently adorned. Great crowds of spectators assembled to witness the scene. Some came in boats upon the water, others took their stations on the shores, where every prominent and commanding point was covered with its own special crowd, and others still occupied the windows of the buildings that looked out upon the river.

Through the midst of this scene the royal barges passed down the river to the Tower. As they moved along, the air was filled with prolonged and continual shouts of "Long live

King Richard!" "Long live the noble Queen Anne!"

Royal or imperial power, once firmly established, will never fail to draw forth the acclamations of the crowd, no matter by what means it has been acquired.

On his arrival at the Tower, Richard was received with great honor by the authorities which he had left in charge there, and he took possession of the edifice formally, as one of his own royal residences. He held a court in the great council-hall. At this court he created several persons peers of the realm, and invested others with the honor of knighthood. These were men whom he supposed to be somewhat undecided in respect to the course which they should pursue, and he wished, by these compliments and honors, to purchase their adhesion to his cause.

He also liberated some persons who had been made prisoners, presuming that, by this kindness, he should conciliate their good-will.

He did not, however, by any means extend this conciliating policy to the case of the young ex-king and his brother; indeed, it would have been extremely dangerous for him to have done so. He was aware that there must be a large number of persons throughout the kingdom

who still considered Edward as the rightful
king, and he knew very well that, if any of
these were to obtain possession of Edward's
person, it would enable them to act vigorously
in his name, and to organize perhaps a powerful party for the support of his claims. He
was convinced, therefore, that it was essential
to the success of his plans that the boys should
be kept in very close and safe custody. So he
removed them from the apartments which they
had hitherto occupied, and shut them up in
close confinement in a gloomy tower upon the
outer walls of the fortress, and which, on account of the cruel murders which were from
time to time committed there, subsequently acquired the name of the Bloody Tower.

Richard and the queen remained at the Tower until the day appointed for the coronation,
which was Tuesday. The ceremonies of that
day were commenced by a grand progress of
the king and his suite through the city of London back to Westminster, only, as if to vary
the pageantry, they went back in grand cavalcade through the streets of the city, instead of
returning as they came, by barges on the river.
The concourse of spectators on this occasion
was even greater than before. The streets were
every where thronged, and very strict regula-

THE BLOODY TOWER.

tions were made, by Richard's command, to prevent disorder.

On arriving at Westminster, the royal party proceeded to the Abbey, where, first of all, as was usual in the case of a coronation, certain ceremonies of religious homage were to be performed at a particular shrine, which was regarded as an object of special sanctity on such occasions. The king and queen proceeded to this shrine from the great hall, barefooted, in token of reverence and humility. They walked, however, it should be added, on ornamented cloth laid down for this purpose on the stone pavements of the floors. All the knights and nobles of England that were present accompanied and followed the king and queen in their pilgrimage to the shrine.

One of these nobles bore the king's crown, another the queen's crown, and others still various other ancient national emblems of royal power. The queen walked under a canopy of silk, with a golden bell hanging from each of the corners of it. The canopy was borne by four great officers of state, and the bells, of course, jingled as the bearers walked along.

The queen wore upon her head a circlet of gold adorned with precious stones. There were four bishops, one at each of the four corners of

the canopy, who walked as immediate attendants upon the queen, and a lady of the very
highest rank followed her, bearing her train.

When the procession reached the shrine, the
king and queen took their seats on each side
of the high altar, and then there came forth a
procession of priests and bishops, clothed in
magnificent sacerdotal robes made of cloth of
gold, and chanting solemn hymns of prayer and
praise as they came.

· After the religious services were completed,
the ceremony of anointing and crowning the
king and queen, and of investing their persons
with the royal robes and emblems, was performed with the usual grand and imposing so-
lemnities.   After this, the royal cortége was
formed again, and the company returned to
Westminster Hall in the same order as they
came.   The queen walked, as before, under her
silken canopy, the golden bells keeping time,
by their tinkling, with the steps of the bearers.

At Westminster Hall a great dais had been
erected, with thrones upon it for the king and
queen. As their majesties advanced and ascended this dais, surrounded by the higher nobles
and chief officers of state, the remainder of the
procession, consisting of those who had come to

accompany and escort them to the place, followed, and filled the hall.

As soon as this vast throng saw that the king and queen were seated upon the dais, with their special and immediate attendants around them, their duties were ended, and they were to be dismissed. A grand officer of state, whose duty it was to dismiss them, came in on horseback, his horse covered with cloth of gold hanging down on both sides to the ground. The people, falling back before this horseman, gradually retired, and thus the hall was cleared.

The king and queen then rose from their seats upon the dais, and were conducted to their private apartments in the palace, to rest and refresh themselves after the fatigues of the public ceremony, and to prepare for the grand banquet which was to take place in the evening.

The preparations for this banquet were made by spreading a table upon the dais under the canopy for the king and queen, and four other very large and long tables through the hall for the invited guests.

The time appointed for the banquet was four o'clock. When the hour arrived, the king and queen were conducted into the hall again, and took their places at the table which had been prepared for them on the dais. They had changed their dresses, having laid aside their royal robes, and the various paraphernalia of office with which they had been induced at the coronation, and now appeared in robes of crimson velvet embroidered with gold, and trimmed with costly furs. They were attended by many lords and ladies of the highest rank, scarcely less magnificently dressed than themselves. They were waited upon, while at table, by the noblest persons in the realm, who served them from the most richly wrought vessels of gold and silver.

After the first part of the banquet was over, a knight, fully armed, and mounted on a warhorse richly caparisoned, rode into the hall, having been previously announced by a herald. This was the king's champion, who came, according to a custom usually observed on such occasions, to challenge and defy the king's enemies, if any such there were.*

The trappings of the champion's horse were of white and red silk, and the armor of the knight himself was bright and glittering. As he rode forward into the area in front of the dais, he called out, in a loud voice, demanding of all present if there were any one there who

* See Frontispiece.

disputed the claim of King Richard the Third to the crown of England.

All the people gazed earnestly at the champion while he made this demand, but no one responded.

The champion then made proclamation again, that if any one there was who would come forward and say that King Richard was not lawfully King of England, he was ready there to fight him to the death, in vindication of Richard's right. As he said this, he threw down his gauntlet upon the floor, in token of defiance.

At this, the whole assembly, with one voice, began to shout, "Long live King Richard!" and the immense hall was filled, for some minutes, with thundering acclamations.

This ceremony being concluded, a company of heralds came forward before the king, and proclaimed "a largesse," as it was called. The ceremony of a largesse consisted in throwing money among the crowd to be scrambled for. Three times the money was thrown out, on this occasion, among the guests in the hall. The amount that is charged on the royal account-book for the expense of this largesse is one hundred pounds.

The scrambling of a crowd for money thrown

9—19

thus among them, one would say, was a very
rude and boisterous amusement, but those were
rude and boisterous times.   The custom holds
its ground in England, in some measure, to the
present day, though now it is confined to throwing out pence and halfpence to the rabble in
the streets at an election, and is no longer, as
of yore, relied upon as a means of entertaining
noble guests at a royal dinner.

After the frolic of the largesse was over, the
king and queen rose to depart.   The evening
was now coming on, and a great number of
torches were brought in to illuminate the hall.
By the light of these torches, the company, after their majesties had retired, gradually withdrew, and the ceremonies of the coronation were
ended.

CHAPTER XV.

THE FATE OF THE PRINCES.

AFTER the coronation, King Richard and Anne, the queen, went to Windsor, and took up their residence there, with the court, for a short time, in order that Richard might attend to the most important of the preliminary arrangements for the management of public affairs, which are always necessary at the commencement of a new reign. As soon as these things were settled, the king set out to make a grand progress through his dominions, for the purpose of receiving the congratulations of the people, and also of impressing them, as much as possible, with a sense of his grandeur and power by the magnificence of his retinue, and the great parades and celebrations by which his progress through the country was to be accompanied.

From Windsor Castle the king went first to Oxford, where he was received with distinguished honors by all the great dignitaries connected with the University. Hence he proceeded to Gloucester, and afterward to Worcester.

19

At all these places he was received with great
parade and pageantry. Those who were disposed to espouse his cause, of course, endeavored to gain his favor by doing all in their power to give éclat to these celebrations. Those
who were indifferent or in doubt, flocked, of
course, to see the shows, and thus involuntarily
contributed to the apparent popularity of the
demonstrations ; while, on the other hand,
those who were opposed to him, and adhered
still secretly to the cause of young King Edward, made no open opposition, but expressed
their dissent, if they expressed it at all, in private conclaves of their own. They could not
do otherwise than to allow Richard to have his
own way during the hour of his triumph, *their*
hour being not yet come.

At last, Richard, in his progress, reached
Warwick Castle, and here he was joined by the
queen and the young prince, who had remained
at Windsor while the king was making his tour
through the western towns, but who now came
across the country with a grand retinue of her
own, to join her husband at her own former
home; for Warwick Castle was the chief stronghold and principal residence of the great Earl
of Warwick, the queen's father.   The king and
queen remained for some time at Warwick

Castle, and the king established his court here, and maintained it with great pomp and splendor. Here he received embassadors from Spain, France, and Burgundy, who had been sent by their several governments to congratulate him on his accession, and to pay him their homage. Each of these embassadors came in great state, and were accompanied by a grand retinue; and the ceremonies of receiving them, and the entertainments given to do them honor, were magnificent beyond description.

One of these embassadors, the one sent by the government of Spain, brought a formal proposal from Ferdinand and Isabella for a marriage between their daughter and Richard's little son. The little prince was at that time about seven years of age.

After remaining some time at Warwick Castle, the royal party proceeded northward, and, after passing through several large towns, they arrived finally at York, which was then, in some sense, the northern capital of the kingdom. Here there was another grand reception. All the nobility and gentry of the surrounding country came in to honor the king's arrival, and the ceremonies attending the entrance of the royal cortége were extremely magnificent.

While the court was at York, Richard repeated the ceremony of the coronation.　On this occasion, his son, the little Prince Edward, was brought forward in a conspicuous manner.　He was created Prince of Wales with great ceremony, and on the day of the coronation he had a little crown upon his head, and his mother led him by the hand in the procession to the altar.

The poor child did not live, however, to realize the grand destiny which his father thus marked out for him.　He died a few months after this at Middleham Castle.

The coronation at York was attended and followed, as that at London had been, with banquets and public parades, and grand celebrations of all sorts, which continued for several successive days, and the hilarity and joy which these shows awakened among the crowds that assembled to witness them seemed to indicate a universal acquiescence on the part of the people of England in Richard's accession to the throne.

Still, although outwardly every thing looked fair, Richard's mind was not yet by any means at ease.　From the very day of his accession, he knew well that, so long as the children of his brother Edward remained alive at the Tower, his seat on the throne could not be secure.　There must necessarily be, he was well aware, a large party in the kingdom who were secretly in favor of Edward, and he knew that they would very soon begin to come to an understanding with each other, and to form plans for effecting a counter-revolution. The most certain means of preventing the formation of these plots, or of defeating them, if formed, would be to remove the children out of the way. He accordingly determined in his heart, before he left London, that this should be done.*

He resolved to put them to death. The deed was to be performed during the course of his royal progress to the north, while the minds of the people of England were engrossed with the splendor of the pageantry with which his progress was accompanied. He intended, moreover, that the murder should be effected in a very secret manner, and that the death of the boys should be closely concealed until a time and occasion should arrive rendering it necessary that it should be made public.

Accordingly, soon after he left London, he sent back a confidential agent, named Green, to

* I say he determined; for, although some of Richard's defenders have denied that he was guilty of the crime which the almost unanimous voice of history charges upon him, the evidence leaves very little room to doubt that the dreadful tale is in all essential particulars entirely true.

Sir Robert Brakenbury, the governor of the Tower, with a letter, in which Sir Robert was commanded to put the boys to death.

Green immediately repaired to London to execute the commission. Richard proceeded on his journey. When he arrived at Warwick, Green returned and joined him there, bringing back the report that Sir Robert refused to obey the order.

Richard was very angry when Green delivered this message. He turned to a page who was in waiting upon him in his chamber, and said, in a rage,

"Even these men that I have brought up and made, refuse to obey my commands."

The page replied,

"Please your majesty, there is a man here in the ante-chamber, that I know, who will obey your majesty's commands, whatever they may be."

Richard asked the page who it was that he meant, and he said Sir James Tyrrel. Sir James Tyrrel was a very talented and accomplished, but very unscrupulous man, and he was quite anxious to acquire the favor of the king. The page knew this, from conversation which Sir James had had with him, and he had been watching an opportunity to recommend

Sir James to Richard's notice, according to an arrangement that Sir James had made with him.

So Richard ordered that Sir James should be sent in. When he came, Richard held a private conference with him, in which he communicated to him, by means of dark hints and insinuations, what he required. Tyrrel undertook to execute the deed. So Richard gave him a letter to Sir Robert Brakenbury, in which he ordered Sir Robert to deliver up the keys of the Tower to Sir James, " to the end," as the letter expressed it, " that he might there accomplish the king's pleasure in such a thing as he had given him commandment."

Sir James, having received this letter, proceeded to London, taking with him such persons as he thought he might require to aid him in his work. Among these was a man named John Dighton. John Dighton was Sir James's groom. He was " a big, broad, square, strong knave," and ready to commit any crime or deed of violence which his master might require. ·

On arriving at the Tower, Sir James delivered his letter to the governor, and the governor gave him up the keys. Sir James went to see the keepers of the prison in which the boys were confined. There were four of them. He

selected from among these four, one, a man
named Miles Forest, whom he concluded to
employ, together with his groom, John Dighton,
to kill the princes.   He formed the plan, gave
the men their instructions, and arranged it with
them that they were to carry the deed into execution that night.

Accordingly, at midnight, when the princes
were asleep, the two men stole softly into the
room, and there wrapped the poor boys up suddenly in the bed-clothes, with pillows pressed
down hard over their faces, so that they could
not breathe.   The boys, of course, were suddenly awakened, in terror, and struggled to get
free; but the men held them down, and kept
the pillows and bed-clothes pressed so closely
over their faces that they could not breathe or
utter any cry.   They held them in this way
until they were entirely suffocated.

When they found that their struggles had
ceased, they slowly opened the bed-clothes and
lifted up the pillows to see if their victims were
really dead.

"Yes," said they to each other, "they are
dead."

The murderers took off the clothes which the
princes had on, and laid out the bodies upon the
bed.   They then went to call Sir James Tyrrel,

who was all ready, in an apartment not far off,
awaiting the summons. He came at once, and,
when he saw that the boys were really dead, he
gave orders that the men should take the bodies
down into the court-yard to be buried.

The grave was dug immediately, just outside
the door, at the foot of the stairs which led up
to the turret in which the boys had been confined. When the bodies had been placed in
the ground, the grave was filled up, and some
stones were put upon the top of it.

Immediately after this work had been accomplished, Sir James delivered back the keys to
the governor of the castle, and mounted his
horse to return to the king. He traveled with
all possible speed, and, on reaching the place
where the king then was, he reported what he
had done.

The king was extremely pleased, and he re-
warded Sir James very liberally for his energy
and zeal ; he, however, expressed some dis-
satisfaction at the manner in which the bodies
had been disposed of. "They should not have
been buried," he said, "in so vile a corner."

So Richard sent word to the governor of the
Tower, and the governor commissioned a priest
to take up the bodies secretly, and inter them
again in a more suitable manner. This priest

soon afterward died, without revealing the
place which he chose for the interment, and so
it was never known where the bodies were
finally laid.

Richard gave all the persons who had been
concerned in this affair very strict instructions
to keep the death of the princes a profound secret. He did not intend to make it known,
unless he should perceive some indication of
an attempt to restore Edward to the throne;
and, had it not been for the occurrence of certain circumstances which will be related in the
next chapter, the fate of the princes might, perhaps, have thus been kept secret for many
years.

QUEEN ELIZABETH AT THE GRAVE OF HER CHILDREN.

CHAPTER XVI.
DOMESTIC TROUBLES.

WHILE Richard was making his triumphal tour through the north of England, apparently receiving a confirmation of his right to the crown by the voice of the whole population of the country, the leaders of the Lancaster party were secretly beginning, in London, to form their schemes for liberating the young princes from the Tower, and restoring Edward to the kingdom.

Queen Elizabeth, who still remained, with the Princess Elizabeth, her oldest daughter, and some of her other children, in the sanctuary at Westminster, was the centre of this movement. She communicated privately with the nobles who were disposed to espouse her cause. The nobles had secret meetings among themselves to form their plans. At these meetings they drank to the health of the king in the Tower, and of his brother, the little Duke of York, and pledged themselves to do every thing in their power to restore the king to his throne. They little knew that the unhappy princes were at

that very time lying together in a corner of the
court-yard of the prison in an ignoble grave.

At length the conspirators' plans were ma-
tured, and the insurrection broke out. Richard immediately prepared to leave York, at the
head of a strong force, to go toward London.
At the same time, he allowed the tidings to be
spread abroad that the two princes were dead.
This news greatly disconcerted the conspirators
and deranged their plans; and when the dreadful intelligence was communicated to the queen
in the sanctuary, she was stunned, and almost
killed by it, as by a blow. "She swooned away,
and fell to the ground, where she lay in great
agony, like a corpse;" and when at length she
was restored to consciousness again, she broke
forth in shrieks and cries of anguish so loud,
that they resounded through the whole Abbey,
and were most pitiful to hear. She beat her
breast and tore her hair, calling all the time to
her children by their names, and bitterly re-
proaching herself for her madness in giving up
the youngest into his enemies' hands. After
exhausting herself with these cries and lamen-
tations, she sank into a state of calm despair,
and, kneeling down upon the floor, she began,
with dreadful earnestness and solemnity, to call
upon Almighty God, imploring him to avenge

the death of her children, and invoking the bitterest curses upon the head of their ruthless murderer.

It was but a short time after this that Richard's child died at Middleham Castle, as stated in the last chapter. Many persons believed that this calamity was a judgment of heaven, brought upon the king in answer to the bereaved mother's imprecations.

It is said that when Queen Elizabeth had recovered a little from the first shock of her grief, she demanded to be taken to her children's grave. So they conducted her to the Tower, and showed her the place in the corner of the court-yard where they had first been buried.

One of the principal leaders of the conspiracy which had been formed against Richard was the Duke of Buckingham—the same that had taken so active a part in bringing Richard to the throne. What induced him to change sides so suddenly is not certainly known. It is supposed that he was dissatisfied with the rewards which Richard bestowed upon him. At any rate, he now turned against the king, and became the leader of the conspirators that were plotting against him.

When the conspirators heard of the death of the princes, they were at first at a loss to

know what to do. They looked about among
the branches of the York and Lancaster families for some one to make their candidate for
the crown. At last they decided upon a certain Henry Tudor, Earl of Richmond. This
Henry, or Richmond, as he was generally called, was descended indirectly from the Lancaster line. The proposal of the conspirators,
however, was, that he should marry the Princess Elizabeth, Queen Elizabeth Woodville's
daughter, who has already been mentioned
among those who fled with their mother to the
sanctuary. Now that both the sons of Elizabeth were dead, this daughter was, of course,
King Edward's next heir, and by her marriage with Richmond the claims of the houses
of York and Lancaster would be, in a measure,
combined.

When this plan was proposed to Queen
Elizabeth, she acceded to it at once, and promised that she would give her daughter in marriage to Richmond, and acknowledge him as
king, provided he would first conquer and depose King Richard, the common enemy.

The plan was accordingly all arranged.
Richmond was in France at this time, having
fled there some time previous, after a battle, in
which his party had been defeated. They

wrote to him, explaining the plan. He immediately fell in with it. He raised a small force —all that he could procure at that time—and set sail, with a few ships, from the port of St. Malo, intending to land on the coast of Devonshire, which is in the southwestern part of England.

In the mean time, the several leaders of the rebellion had gone to different parts of the kingdom, in order to raise troops, and form centres of action against Richard. Buckingham went into Wales. His plan was to march down, with all the forces that he could raise there, to the coast of Devonshire, to meet Richmond on his landing.

This Richard resolved to prevent. He raised an army, and marched to intercept Buckingham. He first, however, issued a proclamation in which he denounced the leaders of the rebellion as criminals and outlaws, and set a price upon their heads.

Buckingham did not succeed in reaching the coast in time to join Richmond. He was stopped by the River Severn, which you will see, by looking on a map of England, came directly in his way. He tried to get across the river, but the people destroyed the bridges and the boats, and he could not get over. He marched up to

20

where the stream was small, in hopes of finding a fording place, but the waters were so swollen with the fall rains that he failed in this attempt as well as the others. The result was, that Richard came up while Buckingham was entangled among the intricacies of the ground produced by the inundations. Buckingham's soldiers, seeing that they were likely to be surrounded, abandoned him and fled. At last Buckingham fled too, and hid himself; but one of his servants came and told Richard where he was. Richard ordered him to be seized. Buckingham sent an imploring message to Richard, begging that Richard would see him, and, before condemning him, hear what he had to say; but Richard, in the place of any reply, gave orders to the soldiers to take the prisoner at once out into the public square of the town, and cut off his head. The order was immediately obeyed.

When Richmond reached the coast of Devonshire, and found that Buckingham was not there to meet him, he was afraid to land with the small force that he had under his command, and so he sailed back to France.

Thus the first attempt made to organize a forcible resistance to Richard's power totally failed.

The unhappy queen, when she heard these
tidings, was once more overwhelmed with grief.
Her situation in the sanctuary was becoming
every day more and more painful. She had
long since exhausted all her own means, and
she imagined that the monks began to think
that she was availing herself of their hospi-
tality too long. Her friends without would
gladly have supplied her wants, but this Richard would not permit. He set a guard around
the sanctuary, and would not allow any one to
come or go. He would starve her out, he said,
if he could not compel her to surrender herself
in any other way.

It was, however, not the queen herself, but
her daughter Elizabeth, who was now the heir
of whatever claims to the throne were possessed
by the family, that Richard was most anxious
to secure. If he could once get Elizabeth into
his power, he thought, he could easily devise
some plan to prevent her marriage with Henry
of Richmond, and so defeat the plans of his enemies in the most effectual manner. He would
have liked still better to have secured Henry
himself; but Henry was in Brittany, on the other side of the Channel, beyond his reach.

He, however, formed a secret plan to get possession of Henry. He offered privately a large

reward to the Duke of Brittany if he would
seize Henry and deliver him into his, Richard's
hands. This the duke engaged to do. But
Henry gained intelligence of the plot before it
was executed, and made his escape from Brittany into France. He was received kindly at
Paris by the French king. The king even
promised to aid him in deposing Richard, and
making himself King of England instead. This
alarmed Richard more than ever.

In the mean time, the summer passed away
and the autumn came on. In November Richard convened Parliament, and caused very severe laws to be passed against those who had
been engaged in the rebellion. Many were executed under these laws, some were banished,
and others shut up in prison. Richard attempted, by these and similar measures, to break down
the spirit of his enemies, and prevent the possibility of their forming any new organizations
against him. Still, notwithstanding all that he
could do, he felt very ill at ease so long as Henry and Elizabeth were at liberty.

At last, in the course of the winter, he conceived the idea of trying what pretended kindness could do in enticing the queen and her
family out of sanctuary. So he sent a messenger to her, to make fair and friendly proposals

to her in case she would give up her place of
refuge and place herself under his protection.
He said that he felt no animosity or ill will
against her, but that, if she and her daughters
would trust to him, he would receive them at
court, provide for them fully in a manner suit-
ed to their rank, and treat them in all respects
with the highest consideration. She herself
should be recognized as the queen dowager of
England, and her daughters as princesses of the
royal family; and he would take proper measures to arrange marriages for the young ladies,
such as should comport with the exalted station which they were entitled to hold.

The queen was at last persuaded to yield to
these solicitations. She left the sanctuary, and
gave herself and her daughters up to Richard's
control. Many persons have censured her very
strongly for doing this; but her friends and defenders allege that there was nothing else that
she could do. She might have remained in the
Abbey herself to starve if she had been alone,
but she could not see her children perish of
destitution and distress when a word from her
could restore them to the world, and raise them
at once to a condition of the highest prosperity
and honor. So she yielded. She left the Abbey, and was established by Richard in one of

his palaces, and her daughters were received at
court, and treated, especially the eldest, with the
utmost consideration.

But, notwithstanding this outward change
in her condition, the real situation of the queen
herself, after leaving the Abbey, was extremely forlorn.   The apartments which Richard assigned to her were very retired and obscure.
He required her, moreover, to dismiss all her
own attendants, and he appointed servants and
agents of his own to wait upon and guard her.
The queen soon found that she was under a
very strict surveillance, and not much less a
prisoner, in fact, than she was before.

While in this situation, she wrote to her son
Dorset,* at Paris, commanding him to put an
end to the proposed marriage of her daughter
Elizabeth to Henry of Richmond, "as she had
given up," she said, "the plan of that alliance,
and had formed other designs for the princess."
Henry and his friends and partisans in Paris
were indignant at receiving this letter, and the
queen has been by many persons much blamed
for having thus broken the engagement which
she had so solemnly made.   Others say that

* The Earl of Dorset, you will recollect, was Queen Elizabeth's son by her first marriage ; he, consequently, had no
claim to the crown.

this letter to Paris was not her free act, but that it was extorted from her by Richard, who had her now completely in his power, and could, of course, easily find means to procure from her any writing that he might desire.

Whether the queen acted freely or not in this case can not certainly be known. At all events, Henry, and those who were acting with him at Paris, determined to regard the letter as written under constraint, and to go on with the maturing of their plans just as if it had never been written.

Richard's plan was, so it was said, to marry the Princess Elizabeth to his own son; for the death of his child, though it has been already once or twice alluded to, had not yet taken place. Richard's son was very young, being at that time about eleven years old; but the princess might be affianced to him, and the marriage consummated when he grew up. Elizabeth herself seems to have fallen in with this proposed arrangement very readily. The prospect that Henry of Richmond would ever succeed in making himself king, and claiming her for his bride, was very remote and uncertain, while Richard was already in full possession of power; and she, by taking his side, and becoming the affianced wife of his son, became at once the first lady in the kingdom, next to Queen Anne, with an apparently certain prospect of becoming queen herself in due time.

But all these fine plans were abruptly brought to an end by the death of the young prince, which occurred about this time, at Middleham Castle, as has been stated before. The death of the poor boy took place in a very sudden and mysterious manner. Some persons supposed that he died by a judgment from heaven, in answer to the awful curses which Queen Elizabeth Woodville imprecated upon the head of the murderer of her children; others thought he was destroyed by poison.

Not very long after the death of the prince, his mother fell very seriously sick. She was broken-hearted at the death of her son, and pining away, she fell into a slow decline. Her sufferings were greatly aggravated by Richard's harsh and cruel treatment of her. He was continually uttering expressions of impatience against her on account of her sickness and uselessness, and making fretful complaints of her various disagreeable qualities. Some of these sayings were reported to Anne, and also a rumor came to her ears one day, while she was at her toilet, that Richard was intending to put her to death. She was dreadfully alarmed at hearing this, and she immediately ran, half dressed as she was, and with her hair disheveled, into the presence of her husband, and, with piteous sobs and bitter tears, asked him what she had done to deserve death. Richard tried to quiet and calm her, assuring her that she had no cause to fear.

She, however, continued to decline; and not long afterward her distress and anguish of mind were greatly increased by hearing that Richard was impatient for her death, in order that he might himself marry the Princess Elizabeth, to whom every one said he was now, since the death of his son, devoting himself personally with great attention. In this state of suffering the poor queen lingered on through the months of the winter, very evidently, though slowly, approaching her end. The universal belief was that Richard had formed the plan of making the Princess Elizabeth his wife, and that the decline and subsequent death of Anne were owing to a slow poison which he caused to be administered to her. There is no proof that this charge was true, but the general belief in the truth of it shows what was the estimate placed, in those times, on Richard's character.

It is very certain, however, that he contemplated this new marriage, and that the princess

herself acceded to the proposed plan, and was
very deeply interested in the accomplishment
of it.   It is said that while the queen still lived
she wrote to one of her friends—a certain noble
duke of high standing and influence—in which
she implored him to aid in forwarding her marriage with the king, whom she called " her
master and her joy in this world—the master
of her heart and thoughts."   In this letter, too,
she expressed her impatience at the queen's
being so long in dying.   " Only think," said
she, " the better part of February is past, and
the queen is still alive.   Will she *never* die?"

But the patience of the princess was not destined to be taxed much longer.   The queen
sank rapidly after this, and in March she died.

The heart of Elizabeth was now filled with
exultation and delight.   The great obstacle to
her marriage with her uncle was now removed,
and the way was open before her to become a
queen.   It is true that the relationship which
existed between her and Richard, that of uncle
and niece, was such as to make the marriage
utterly illegal.   But Richard had a plan of ob-
taining a dispensation from the Pope, which he
had no doubt that he could easily do, and a
dispensation from the Pope, according to the
ideas of those times, would legalize any thing.

So Richard cautiously proposed his plan to some of his confidential counselors.

His counselors told him that the execution of such a plan would be dangerous in the highest degree. The people of England, they said, had for some time been led to think that the king had that design in contemplation, and that the idea had awakened a great deal of indignation throughout the country. The land was full of rumors and murmurings, they said, and those of a very threatening character. The marriage would be considered incestuous both by the clergy and the people, and would be looked upon with abhorrence. Besides, they said, there were a great many dark suspicions in the minds of the people that Richard had been himself the cause of the death of his former wife Anne, in order to open the way for this marriage, and now, if the marriage were really to take place, all these suspicions would be confirmed. They could judge somewhat, they added, by the depth of the excitement which had been produced by the bare suspicion that such things were contemplated, how great would be the violence of the outbreak of public indignation if the design were carried into effect. Richard would be in the utmost danger of losing his kingdom.

PORTRAIT OF THE PRINCESS ELIZABETH.

So Richard determined at once to abandon
the plan. He caused it to be announced in the
most public manner that he had never contemplated such a marriage, and that all the rumors
attributing such a design to him were malicious

and false. He also sent orders abroad throughout the kingdom requiring that all persons who had circulated such rumors should be arrested and sent to London to be punished.

Elizabeth's hopes were, of course, suddenly blasted, and the splendid castle which her imagination had built fell to the ground. It was only a temporary disappointment, however, for she became Queen of England in the end, after all.

CHAPTER XVII.

THE FIELD OF BOSWORTH.

IN the mean time, while Richard had been
occupied with the schemes and manœuvres
described in the last chapter, Richmond was going on steadily in Paris with the preparations
that he was making for a new invasion of England. The King of France assisted him both
by providing him with money and aiding him
in the enlistment of men. When Richmond
received the message from Elizabeth's mother
declaring that the proposed match between him
and the princess must be broken off, and heard
that Richard had formed a plan for marrying
the young lady himself, he paid no regard to
the tidings, but declared that he should proceed
with his plans as vigorously as ever, and that,
whatever counter-schemes they might form,
they might rely upon it that he should fully
carry into effect his purpose, not only of deposing Richard and reigning in his stead, but also
of making the Princess Elizabeth his wife, according to his original intention.

At length the expedition was ready, and the

fleet conveying it set sail from the port of Harfleur.

Richard attempted to arouse the people of England against the invaders by a grand proclamation which he issued. In this proclamation he designated the Earl of Richmond as "one Henry Tudor," who had no claim whatever, of any kind, to the English throne, but who was coming to attempt to seize it without any color of right. In order to obtain assistance from the King of France, he had promised, the proclamation said, "to surrender to him, in case he was successful, all the rich possessions in France which at that time belonged to England, even Calais itself; and he had promised, moreover, and given away, to the traitors and foreigners who were coming with him, all the most important and valuable places in the kingdom—archbishoprics, bishoprics, duchies, earldoms, baronies, and many other inheritances belonging of right to the English knights, esquires, and gentlemen who were now in the possession of them. The proclamation farther declared that the people who made up his army were robbers and murderers, and rebels attainted by Parliament, many of whom had made themselves infamous as cutthroats, adulterers, and extortioners."

9—21

Richard closed his proclamation by calling upon all his subjects to arm themselves, like true and good Englishmen, for the defense of their wives, children, goods, and hereditaments, and he promised that he himself, like a true and courageous prince, would put himself in the forefront of the battle, and expose his royal person to the worst of the dangers that were to be incurred in the defense of the country.

At the same time that he issued this proclamation, Richard sent forth orders to all parts of the kingdom, commanding the nobles and barons to marshal their forces, and make ready to march at a moment's warning. He dispatched detachments of his forces to the southward to defend the southern coast, where he expected Richmond would land, while he himself proceeded northward, toward the centre of the kingdom, to assemble and organize his grand army. He made Nottingham his headquarters, and he gradually gathered around him, in that city, a very large force.

In the mean time, while these movements and preparations had been going on on both sides, the spring and the early part of the summer passed away, and at length Richard, at Nottingham, in the month of August, received the tidings that Richmond had landed at Milford

Haven, on the southwestern coast of Wales, with a force of two or three thousand men. Richard said that he was glad to hear it. " I am glad," said he, " that at last he has come. I have now only to meet him, and gain one de- cisive victory, and then the security of my kingdom will be disturbed no more."

Richmond did not rely wholly on the troops which he had brought with him for the success of his cause. He believed that there was a great and prevailing feeling of disaffection against Richard throughout England, and that, as soon as it should appear that he, Richmond, was really in earnest in his determination to claim and take the crown, and that there was a rea- sonable prospect of the success of his enterprise, great numbers of men, who were now ostensi- bly on Richard's side, would forsake him and join the invader. So he sent secret messen- gers throughout the kingdom to communicate with his friends, and to open negotiations with those of Richard's adherents who might possi- bly be inclined to change sides. In order to give time for these negotiations to produce their effect, he resolved not to march at once into the interior of the country, but to proceed slowly toward the eastward, along the southern coast of Wales, awaiting intelligence. This plan he pursued. His strength increased rapidly as he advanced. At length, when he reached the eastern borders of Wales, he began to feel strong enough to push forward into England to meet Richard, who was all this time gathering his forces together at Nottingham, and preparing for a very formidable resistance of the invader. He accordingly advanced to Leicester, and thence to the town of Tamworth, where there was a strong castle on a rock. He took possession of this castle, and made it, for a time, his head-quarters.

In the mean time, Richard, having received intelligence of Richmond's movements, and having now made every thing ready for his own advance, determined to delay no longer, but to go forth and meet his enemy. Accordingly, one morning, he marshaled his troops in the market-place of Nottingham, "separating his foot-soldiers in two divisions, five abreast, and dividing his cavalry so as to form two wide-spreading wings." He placed his artillery, with the ammunition, in the centre, reserving for himself a position in a space immediately behind it.

When all was ready, he came out from the castle mounted upon a milk-white charger. He wore, according to the custom of the times, a

THE CASTLE AT TAMWORTH.

very magnificent armor, resplendent with gold
and embroidery, and with polished steel that
glittered in the sun. Over his helmet he wore
his royal crown. He was preceded and followed, as he came out through the castle gates and
descended the winding way which led down
from the hill on which the castle stands, by
guards splendidly dressed and mounted—arch-
ers, and spearmen, and other men at arms—
with ensigns bearing innumerable pennants and
banners. As soon as he joined the army in the
town the order was given to march, and so great
was the number of men that he had under his
command that they were more than an hour
in marching out of Nottingham, and when all
had finally issued from the gate, the column
covered the road for three miles.

At length, after some days of manœuvring
and marching, the two armies came into the immediate vicinity of each other near the town
of Bosworth, at a place where there was a wide
field, which has since been greatly renowned in
history as the Field of Bosworth. The two
armies advanced into the neighborhood of this
field on the 19th and 20th days of August, and
both sides began to prepare for battle.

The army which Richard commanded was
far more numerous and imposing than that of

Richmond, and every thing, so far as outward
appearances were concerned, promised him an
easy victory. And yet Richmond was exultant
in his confidence of success, while Richard was
harassed with gloomy forebodings. His mind
was filled with perplexity and distress. He believed that the leading nobles and generals on
his side had secretly resolved to betray him,
and that they were prepared to abandon him
and go over to the enemy on the very field of
battle, unless he could gain advantages so decisive at the very commencement of the conflict as to show that the cause of Richmond was
hopeless. Although Richard was morally convinced that this was the state of things, he had
no sufficient evidence of it to justify his taking
any action against the men that he suspected.
He did not even dare to express his suspicions,
for he knew that if he were to do so, or even
to intimate that he felt suspicion, the only effect would be to precipitate the consummation
of the treachery that he feared, and perhaps
drive some to abandon him who had not yet
fully resolved on doing so. He was obliged,
therefore, though suffering the greatest anxiety
and alarm, to suppress all indications of his un-
easiness, except to his most confidential friends.
To them he appeared, as one of them stated,

"sore moved and broiled with melancholy and dolor, and from time to time he cried out, asking vengeance of them that, contrary to their oath and promise, were so deceiving him."

The recollection of the many crimes that he had committed in the attainment of the power which he now feared he was about to lose forever, harassed his mind and tormented his conscience, especially at night. "He took ill rest at nights," says one of his biographers, "using to lie long, waking and musing, sore wearied with care and watch, and rather slumbered than slept, troubled with fearful dreams."

On the day of the battle Richard found the worst of his forebodings fulfilled. In the early part of the day he took a position upon an elevated portion of the ground, where he could survey the whole field, and direct the movements of his troops. From this point he could see, as the battle went on, one body of men after another go over to the enemy. He was overwhelmed with vexation and rage. He cried out, Treason! Treason! and, calling upon his guards and attendants to follow him, he rushed down the hill, determined to force his way to the part of the field where Richmond himself was stationed, with a view of engaging him and killing him with his own hand. This, he thought, was the last hope that was now left him.

There was a spring of water, and a little brook flowing from it in a part of the field where he had to pass. He stopped at this spring, opened his helmet, and took a drink of the water. He then closed his helmet and rode on.

This spring afterward received, from this circumstance, the name of "Richard's Well," and it is known by that name to this day.

From the spring Richard rushed forward, attended by a few followers as fearless as himself, in search of Richmond. He penetrated the enemies' lines in the direction where he supposed Richmond was to be found, and was soon surrounded by foes, whom he engaged desperately in a hand-to-hand encounter of the most furious and reckless character. He slew one or two of the foremost of those who surrounded him, calling out all the time to Richmond to come out and meet him in single combat. This Richmond would not do. In the mean time, many of Richard's friends came up to his assistance. Some of these urged him to retire, saying that it was useless for him to attempt to maintain so unequal a contest, but he refused to go.

"Not one foot will I fly," said he, "so long as breath bides within my breast; for, by Him that shaped both sea and land, this day shall end my battles or my life. I will die King of England."

So he fought on. Several faithful friends still adhered to him and fought by his side. His standard-bearer stood his ground, with the king's banner in his hand, until at last both his legs were cut off under him, and he fell to the earth; still he would not let the banner go, but clung to it with a convulsive grasp till he died.

At last Richard too was overpowered by the numbers that beset him. Exhausted by his exertions, and weakened by loss of blood, he was beaten down from his horse to the ground and killed. The royal crown which he had worn so proudly into the battle was knocked from his head in the dreadful affray, and trampled in the dust.

Lord Stanley, one of the chieftains who had abandoned Richard's cause and gone over to the enemy, picked up the crown, all battered and bloodstained as it was, and put it upon Richmond's head. From that hour Richmond was recognized as King of England. He reigned under the title of Henry the Seventh.

KING HENRY VII.

The few followers that had remained faithful
to Richard's cause up to this time now gave
up the contest and fled. The victors lifted up
the dead body of the king, took off the armor,
and then placed the body across the back of a
horse, behind a pursuivant-at-arms, who, thus
mounted, rode a little behind the new king as

he retired from the field of battle. Followed by this dreadful trophy of his victory, King Henry entered the town of Leicester in triumph. The body of Richard was exposed for three days, in a public place, to the view of all beholders, in order that every body might be satisfied that he was really dead, and then the new king proceeded by easy journeys to London. The people came out to meet him all along the way, receiving him every where with shouts and acclamations, and crying, "King Henry! King Henry! Long live our sovereign lord, King Henry!"

For several weeks after his accession Henry's mind was occupied with public affairs, but, as soon as the most urgent of the calls upon his attention were disposed of, he renewed his proposals to the Princess Elizabeth, and in January of the next year they were married. It seems to have been a matter of no consequence to her whether one man or another was her husband, provided he was only King of England, so that she could be queen. Henry's motive, too, in marrying her, was equally mercenary, his only object being to secure to himself, through her, the right of inheritance to her father's claims to the throne. He accordingly never pretended to feel any love for her, and, after his marriage, he treated her with great coldness and neglect.

His conduct toward her poor mother, the dowager queen, Elizabeth Woodville, was still more unfriendly. He sent her to a gloomy monastery, called the Monastery of Bermond-sey, and caused her to be kept there in the custody of the monks, virtually a prisoner. The reason which he assigned for this was his displeasure with her for abandoning his cause, and breaking the engagement which she had made with him for the marriage of her daughter to him, and also for giving herself and her daughter up into Richard's hands, and joining with him in the intrigues which Richard formed for connecting the princess with his family. In this lonely retreat the widowed queen passed the remainder of her days. She was not precisely a prisoner—at least, she was not kept in close and continual confinement, for two or three times, in the course of the few remaining years that she lived, she was brought, on special occasions, to court, and treated there with a certain degree of attention and respect. One of these occasions was that of the baptism of her daughter's child.

In this lonely and cheerless retreat the queen lingered a few years, and then died. Her body

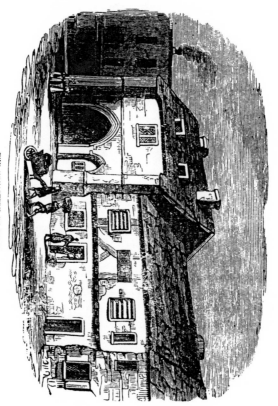

THE MONASTERY OF BERMONDSEY.

was conveyed to Windsor for interment, and her daughters and the friends of her family were notified of the event. A very few came to attend the funeral. Her daughter Elizabeth was indisposed, and did not come. The interment took place at night. A few poor old men, in tattered garments, were employed to officiate at the ceremony by holding " old torches and torches' ends" to light the gloomy precincts of the chapel during the time while the monks were chanting the funeral dirge.

9—22

THE END.

COSIMO is a specialty publisher of books and publications that inspire, inform, and engage readers. Our mission is to offer unique books to niche audiences around the world.

COSIMO BOOKS publishes books and publications for innovative authors, nonprofit organizations, and businesses. **COSIMO BOOKS** specializes in bringing books back into print, publishing new books quickly and effectively, and making these publications available to readers around the world.

COSIMO CLASSICS offers a collection of distinctive titles by the great authors and thinkers throughout the ages. At **COSIMO CLASSICS** timeless works find new life as affordable books, covering a variety of subjects including: Business, Economics, History, Personal Development, Philosophy, Religion & Spirituality, and much more!

COSIMO REPORTS publishes public reports that affect your world, from global trends to the economy, and from health to geopolitics.

LaVergne, TN USA
02 December 2009
165786LV00004B/8/P